EAT.SLEEP.WALK. REPEAT

A journey of 500 miles home

GRACE ALSANCAK-HAY

To Auntie Sue & Uncle David

Thanks for the support!

Hope you enjoy the book

Lots of love

Grace :)

xxx

ISBN: 9798681239321

DEDICATION

To Mum and Dad

Mum, your strength and determination to get through these trying years is nothing short of inspiring. You have handled everything that has been thrown at you in such a positive light and always carried on fighting. You're an inspiration! Thank you for being you and always supporting me in whatever crazy thing I decide to do next.

Dad, the past few years have been a challenge for us all, but you have remained a constant pillar of support for us as a family. Thank you for everything and for always being the sounding board and number 1 fan for my ideas. You are stronger then you know!

To Joe

Never stop being you

To Phil

Thank you for putting up with me and sacrificing our honeymoon to complete this journey. While I will never forgive you for planting this idea in my head (don't even try to deny it) I will always be grateful for all the physical and mental support you gave me throughout. My partner in crime, I couldn't have done it without you! Thank you for being my rock…and I promise you will get a copy of THIS book!

To my feet

I'm sorry I put you through this…

CHAPTERS

Maps of our walking route

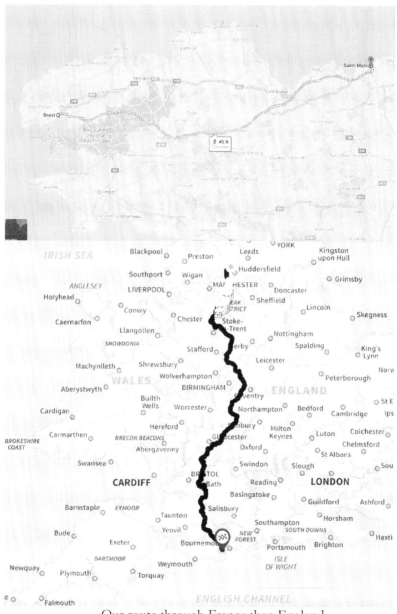

Our route through France then England

GRACE ALSANCAK-HAY

CHAPTER 1: THE TEAM

Grace: Age 27 at the start of the walk, Grace works full time as springboard and platform diving coach in Southend on Sea. Originally from Halifax in West Yorkshire she spent 5 years at Leeds Beckett University where she met Phil who 9 years later would become her husband. Spending many years as a diver herself in her home town she was squad mates with Rachael and they have remained friends ever since, regularly coming together to plot their next crazy adventure whether it be bungee jumping, climbing Mount Kilimanjaro or rolling down a hill in a giant inflatable zorb you will often find them both doing it together. Not a stranger to a charity challenge in the summer of 2014 Grace was part of a two-man team who kayaked the length of the Mississippi river in America and raised £70,000+ for charity.

Dean: 43 at the start of the walk, Dean is a qualified Massage Therapist who's list of physical feats and achievements knows no end. A keen cyclist he has completed Lands' End to John O Groats, multiple coast to coast trips as well as the Pyrenees on two wheels. On top of this he has twice cycled 256 miles non-stop for an Audax Cycle Event. Dean also enjoys running and whether it be across moor land, mountains or roads he has raced on it all. No stranger to full or half marathons Dean is often seen with Rachael planning their next long-distance adventure.

Rachael: Age 28 years old when the team set out for France, Rachael has packed a lot into her time so far. After studying at university in Leeds she volunteered at the London and Rio Summer Olympic and Paralympic Games as well as the Sochi Winter games in 2018. Not new to adventures, Rachael summited Kilimanjaro alongside Grace in 2011, then went on to trek to Everest Base Camp followed by climbing Mount Aconcagua in Argentina. Also a keen cyclist and runner Rachael often teams up with Dean to find the next interesting run or cycle be it in the UK or abroad.

Phil: Celebrating his 28th birthday days before setting out for France, Phil is an Automotive Photographer by trade working self-employed in the UK and Europe. www.philhayphotography.com. Born and raised on the North Yorkshire moors, Phil then moved to Leeds to study at university where he met Grace, and well the rest is history. A keen kayaker and traveler Phil always has his camera with him to capture the moment and he acted as resident photographer for Quest for Brest.

CHAPTER 2: THE 'C' WORD

It was one afternoon in the summer of 2018 when the 'c word' was first mentioned.

I was up home in Elland for a few days (having travelled up from Southend on Sea where I lived at the time) before going on a family holiday for a week in Cornwall, starting Sunday 19.08.18. My Mum and I had spent a lovely day in Leeds along with three of my close friends on Thursday 16.08.18 choosing bridesmaid dresses for my wedding in June 2019. We'd had a great time. It was now lunchtime on Saturday 18.08.18 and Phil (now my husband) and I had decided we would cook lunch for everyone as my Mum, Dad and Brother were setting off on their journey down to Cornwall that same evening.

Phil and I were in the kitchen cutting up spring onions to make some salt and pepper chicken when my Mum and Dad came into the kitchen. My Mum told us they would have to leave the forthcoming holiday a few days early. I turned and looked at her, trying to read her face and to understand what was going on. My Mum simply looked at me and said

"A few days ago I found a lump under my arm. I've been to see my Doctor and I have to go and get it checked out. The first appointment they could offer me is in Huddersfield on Friday which I had to accept so we will need to leave Cornwall early.

I was instantly hit with a sinking feeling in my stomach. Everyone knows what a lump could mean. Did my Mum have cancer? 'Its probably nothing' she said, 'I've been going to all my scans and I had a biopsy done not that long ago and it all came back clear, so I'm sure it will be fine but I just have to go and have it looked at'.

As much as I wanted to be as optimistic as my Mum my head was instantly filled with the thought of what if it is cancer and what if my Mum is going to die. Phil and I were due to get married in June 2019, what if my Mum wasn't going to be there? What if it was cancer and she was told it was incurable? How could I help? What could I do?

I just put my head in my hands and simply began to cry, all over the spring onions. It felt to be ages before anyone spoke again. I looked up and saw my Dad stood in the corner of the room with his head down clearly holding back the tears. Both my parents' Mums (and therefore my grandmas) had passed away from cancer at a young age and now here it was again rearing its ugly head to ruin another generation!

How you move on from being told something like that and continue with your day to day life is difficult. My excitement for the forthcoming holiday had disappeared. I was due to attend the "evening do" of a school friend's wedding that evening but my desire to party and celebrate completely disappeared. I just wanted to sit with my Mum and Dad and at least try to pretend that everything was normal and okay. However, I didn't do this, I couldn't miss my friend's special celebration, so I tried to put the thoughts to the back of my head and we attended the party. I was there in person but not in mind. Old school friends asked me "how are your parents?" I had to reply with "they are both doing really well" to avoid awkward questions that I was unable to answer and to avoid spoiling everyone's day. It was extremely hard to put on a brave face when all I wanted to do was cry.

We all went to Cornwall to start our holiday, my parents, my brother, and Phil's parents. It served as a great distraction from the "elephant in the room"!

As planned, my parents and brother left a few days early to enable my Mum and Dad to attend "the appointment". Meanwhile Phil and I, along with his parents, stayed in Cornwall to complete our holiday.

The day of the appointment came around quickly and I was on tenterhooks all day. We were shopping in Tesco's in Truro when the dreaded phone call came from my Mum. I headed outside; If it was bad news, I didn't want to be crying in the poultry aisle! I answered the phone to hear my Mum saying "I'm afraid it's bad news, it is cancer and its quite a sizable lump. They can't say too much right now, but it's more than likely going to be the full works of chemotherapy, probably an operation followed by radiotherapy." I slumped to the floor and just cried. It wasn't just a bad dream! My Mum had cancer.

The next 12 months would be nothing short of challenging. Living 200+ miles away from my family made me feel pretty useless throughout the whole process. I knew my Dad was struggling; helping your wife through cancer while still looking after your son who has autism and severe developmental delay is not the easiest situation for anyone to deal with. Thankfully my wider family rallied round my Mum and Dad, helping to fill the roles I was unable to do and for that I will be forever grateful.

I went home as often as possible, but each trip became harder and harder as I saw my Mum deteriorate into what can only be described as a shell of her former self. The chemotherapy was taking its toll and there wasn't anything I could really do to help.

One moment that hit me hard was when I was back at home for a weekend to attend a diving competition in Leeds. I had arrived home on the Thursday evening so I could take Mum to her chemotherapy session on the Friday morning. It helped me to see that she was in no pain during her chemotherapy but sitting there and seeing so many people come in and out of the unit (almost like a conveyor belt) was heart breaking. I spent that same evening helping Mum try out the scarves she had been given to wear if she lost her hair as a result of her treatment; not something you ever expect to have to do as a daughter and one that hit me hard.

I tried to remain as positive as possible for my Mum and Dad, and helped where I could, but life had to continue. Each time I left home to go back to Southend on Sea and my life down there, I was worried about how my Mum would look the next time I saw her. Only being able to see her once a month or so made the changes even more shocking and hard to see.

CHAPTER 3: THE PLAN

From the date my Mum was diagnosed with Cancer, I, just like anyone else I imagine, felt helpless. I wished I could do more to help.

In my time I have undertaken various challenges for charity the most demanding ones being climbing Mount Kilimanjaro, and Kayaking 2350 miles of the Mississippi River. If I could find a new challenge to do whilst raising money for a cancer-based Charity at the same time, maybe this was a way I could help. I certainly couldn't take the pain and suffering away from my Mum, but a charity devoted to helping those with cancer could go a long way to do doing so.

So, fast forward a few months to a mini break me and Phil had taken to Vienna and a conversation we were having regarding the above. We were racking our brains trying to think of a challenge to do but nothing was inspiring us. A few minutes later Phil simply said

'Wait a minute, isn't there a place in France called Brest? Why don't you walk back from there or something?" I sat and thought for a moment, it seemed plausible, crazy but still plausible. I sat and let the idea roll around in my head. It sounded like a good idea and was the only thing that had made me stop and really think about it....... a genuine idea! Well that was it, the idea had been sown, and began to take root. I would walk home from France. Now all I needed was team of others also crazy enough to think this was a good idea. Who would accept this challenge alongside me?

The name Rachael Bradley suddenly entered my head. A long-time friend from my diving days. There and then I sent Rachael a text that simply said, "I'm thinking of doing a walk for charity in the summer of next year, a long walk, are you in?" Before long I had my reply, "Yes I'm in, no questions asked." The team for the challenge was starting to take shape.

I knew Rachael would be the perfect type of team member for this challenge, having not only done Kilimanjaro with me she was also a veteran of Everest base camp, multiple long-distance bike rides and runs and not to mention as bonkers as me to think that this was a great idea.

Next step was to decide on which particular charity we would raise money for. I asked my mum if there was a particular charity who she felt had been a real help to her so far and therefore would be good to raise money for, she chose Macmillan Cancer Support.

CHAPTER 4: PLANNING AND PREPERATION

Where do you even begin when it comes to planning a route for a walk of around 500 miles, I hear you ask. You sit and trawl through online and paper maps of course.

Once home from Vienna the first thing I did was begin researching our idea. Had anyone walked this route before? Would there be footpaths and national trails all the way through the route? The answer to these were "no" and "not quite".

I researched all the different national trails and their locations in relation to Halifax. I stumbled across a website by a couple who had walked from Lands' End to John O Groats during their retirement. Their website listed all the different trails they had used, and I thought this could be a good place to start. We wouldn't need all the routes of course but I could simply look at what they used to get from the south coast to somewhere near Halifax, and then build a picture of where we could walk.

The Cotswold Way, Heart of England Way, and Staffordshire Way were just some of the trails we would need, and these could get us as far south as Bath. The next question was where to cross the English Channel? The go to answer for most people would be Calais, however this would mean crossing to the east side of England, adding on hundreds of miles, and then adding on further miles still walking from Calais to Brest on the north-west coast of France. This needed to be a realistic challenge and one that wouldn't take months to complete. I needed to think this through carefully!

A quick search via "google" told me ferries regularly cross from Poole to St Malo. Given that Poole lies directly south of Bath and St Malo a lot closer to Brest than Callais, this seemed like a good option. Excellent, now I just needed to find a route from Bath down to the ferry port in Poole.

Ordinance Survey have an online mapping service that allows you access to every map of the British Isles in return for a payment of £25, this seemed perfect and would be a great way to begin plotting a route.

After a few months I had managed to use the online map service alongside versions of the paper maps to create a route from Halifax all the way down to Poole, using as many national trails as possible (after all we couldn't exactly walk up the motorways), and averaging between 15 and 20 miles a day. I had to use paper maps as well because the "zoom" I needed to use on the online maps to pick up enough details meant I had no idea what was around me or the direction I was aiming to travel in. I followed a process of laying out each map on the floor and plotted simultaneously onto the computer and paper to ensure I was always heading in the correct direction to join up with the next required trail. It was a long and laborious process. Phil would regularly arrive home to see our living room floor strewn with maps!

Alongside planning a route, I also started to jot down ideas of the type of kit we would need. I already had a large amount of hiking gear from climbing Kilimanjaro and completing my Bronze and Silver Duke of Edinburgh Awards, but this would be a challenge on another level and I needed to be prepared. I trawled through hours and hours of "YouTube" footage of reviews and advice on good gear for long distance hikes.

It was during this time that Rachael asked if her friend Dean could join us, the answer was a definite yes, after all my thinking was the more the merrier and each person would be able to bring a different dynamic and their own experiences to the fore. We decided it was probably a good idea to meet up sometime soon to talk through ideas and the progress we had already made. Moving forward to the December of 2018, myself, Phil, Rachael and Dean were sat around the dining room table in my parent's house pouring over the maps I had plotted a route on. We would all need to take unpaid leave from work to undertake this challenge, so getting the time needed to achieve it correct was important. We had to be realistic about what mileage we could manage each day. We settled on 20 miles a day, walking a minimum of 2 miles per hour. This would mean we needed to walk approximately 10 hours a day. Whilst it could be done, we all agreed it would be better to aim to walk around 3 miles per hour so that we still had plenty time to rest up. One thing I had learnt from my "Mississippi experience" was how vital it was to plan in contingency days for injury or simply time for recovery when we had found we had bitten of more that we could chew. On the river, for whatever reason, we hadn't really taken this type of thing into account, so I wasn't going to let that happen this time.

I suggested we go with a pattern of walking 3 or 4 days and then have a day off. Some people may read this and think when put like that it sounds like it was going to be easy, but however hard I knew this was going to be I did want to try and enjoy it in some capacity. We would be walking through towns and cities I had never seen before and even though we wouldn't have time to explore each and every one, a few days in and amongst the walking to explore and rest up would go a long way towards making this achievable on both a physical and mental level. In hindsight, having completed this walk, I think this was my best decision and I'm glad I stood by it.

A plan was coming together, and we now even had a title. We decided to name the challenge Quest to Brest. We continued on in our discussions throwing ideas back and forth across the table when my Dad (who had come to join us for a bit) did what my Dad does best and came out with a simple but obvious statement that threw a spanner in the works.

"I don't mean to interrupt but why don't you do it the other way around and walk from France to Halifax. I'm sure you would then get a much better reception at the "finish line" rather than it just being the four of you in France". We all looked at each other as it dawned on us that what my Dad was saying was a great idea. So, the decision was made there and then to do the walk the other way around, walking from Brest back to Halifax.

While my Dad's idea was brilliant it did mean re-planning the entire route day by day! Yes, we could have followed the route the other way around, but the ascent and descent would now change which could affect the length of the day or time needed to achieve them. In addition, the routes would also need to be the right way around to ensure we could follow them correctly on a "Garmin". So, it was back to the beginning for the route planning. The joys! We also needed to re-think the name of our challenge as we would no longer be walking to Brest, hence the name becoming "Quest for Brest" instead.

Given how long it had already taken me to plan the English section of the route, Dean and Rachael said they would take home the French maps and start looking into plotting a route from Brest to St Malo.

Once we returned home to Southend it was back to the drawing board and pouring over maps late into the night to try and get a route finalised. I then spent some time designing a logo and website that would help us kick start some interest in what we were doing. It soon became a case of all my free time being thrown into either wedding or walk planning.

I made contact with members of the Macmillan Cancer Support team down south who agreed to help us promote what we were doing and provided us with t shirts for promotional photos. My dad was on a mission back up home to set up a big finish for us as he also made contact with the local Macmillan team. On a visit home I met with him and a member of their team called Adele, and between us we came up with the idea of finishing at the Piece

Hall, a grade 1 listed building that acts as a center piece to the town of Halifax. Adele and the team from Macmillan kept in frequent touch with us providing publicity and advice throughout the planning which was a great help.

It was now 4 months into my Mum's weekly chemotherapy treatment. It had really "kicked in" and was taking its toll on her both physically and mentally. She was spending much of her day in bed, too tired to do anything. She had become a shell of her former self.   It was extremely hard to see someone you love so dearly become almost unrecognisable in terms of personality. I had such limited conversation with her during my short time at home through the Christmas period in 2018 and even the ones we did have were short in duration. She was unaware of a lot of what was happening around her at this time however, one morning she did manage to come and tell me quite forcibly that she didn't want me to do this walk and that she felt it was a bad idea. I realised it was the drugs and medication talking as only a month ago she had told me how proud she was of me undertaking such a thing, but it still hurt me to hear her say it.

At several points during the same holiday my Mum repeated what she had said to me. I began to question whether I should be doing this. I felt angry, not at my Mum but at what the chemotherapy was doing to her, this whole idea had started because I wanted to do something more to help my Mum and now, she was the one telling me not to do it. I put the thought to the back of my mind and carried on planning in the hope that once treatment was over and 'chemo Mum' left us things would return to normal.

CHAPTER 5: LOOSING WEIGHT

Over the coming months prior to the challenge I was beginning to put together a pretty detailed and thought out list of what we would need to carry. Weight was going to play a major part during the trip; it would need to be kept to the bare minimum to help us both physically and mentally.

Previous challenges, involving carrying a rucksack, had taught me that carrying too much weight will really weigh you down (pun intended)! I thought back to when I summited Kilimanjaro. My main bag had weighed in at 13kg (28lbs), and the small day bag I had carried with me was around 7kg. The latter had no food in it and with only enough water to get me through a morning or afternoon that was quite heavy. That had been a combined total of 20kg (44lbs)! Things would definitely have to change for this challenge. I set an ambitious target of keeping the weight I would be carrying to just over 10kg (22lbs), inclusive of food and water.

At first it seemed it would be simple to lose a big chunk of weight, after all I wouldn't be taking an artic type sleeping bag or layer and layers of thick and heavy clothing, however I would have to carry a tent which was something I hadn't had to do up Kilimanjaro. There was only one thing for it I was going to have to be ruthless with my kit and this is where an obsession with weight began.

I wrote out a list of everything I thought I would need to take with me, marking off those I already had. While our budget for this challenge was minimal there were key bits of equipment that needed to be bought.

An essential piece of equipment was my rucksack. I had my 65-litre rucksack from summiting Kilimanjaro and my original plan was to simply use this as it was nice and big, however I was thrown back to the memories of how heavy that bag had felt whilst carrying it, so I decided to weigh it. I wasn't particularly shocked to find that the bag weighed 2.7kg (5.9lbs) when empty. Given that my aim was to carry around 10 kg (22lbs) this only left me with 7.3kg (16lbs) for contents.

I needed a tent. The 2 man tent I had carried in my kayak down the Mississippi weighed 2.8kg (6.7lbs). Splitting the weight in half between myself and Phil in France meant carrying 1.4kg (3lbs) each and this seemed reasonable but carrying that all by myself once we got to England would increase my weight to 5.5kg (12lbs) and that was only my tent and rucksack. This was impossible.

(Phil would only be joining us for the section of the walk in France due to work commitments, he would join us on his days off in England but for the most of it there would just be 3 of us.)

I devoted hours and hours into researching reasonably priced, good quality lightweight tents and rucksacks that wouldn't break the bank. It gradually became apparent I didn't need anywhere near 65 litres of space to carry everything in fact it was advised somewhere around 50 litres would be ample. I was sceptical at first but rationalised it as a way of ensuring I wouldn't carry anything unnecessarily. If "push came to shove" I could always strap bulkier items onto the outside of the rucksack. I purchased the Osprey Eja 48 litre woman's rucksack. A fantastic bit of equipment that came in at a weight of 1.17kg (2.5lbs). Brilliant, rucksack sorted; it was time to source a lighter tent. I trawled websites and contacted hire companies to find a tent that was lightweight, inexpensive, roomy and preferably free standing. On the Mississippi we had ended up at a few campsites where the ground had been so hard it was impossible for the pegs to go into the ground properly. The tent was held up by two poles running parallel to each other rather than the "criss-cross" shape of a standard off the shelf festival tent and this meant that without pegs held securely in the ground it would simply fall over. We didn't want this to happen! I found a tent that seemed fit for purpose and ticked most boxes. It was the Sierra Designs High Side. It was lightweight, had porch space and was in the sale with £150 off! I snapped it up for a grand total of £90. Weighing in at 1.11kg (2.4lbs) this was perfect for the English section of the walk. I had spent my time (and money) well. My basic weight was now only 2.28kg (5lbs) leaving me a good 7+kg (15lbs) to play with. Given the additional weight of food and water I decided I needed to aim for all my other kit/luggage to weigh under 8kg (17lbs). This still allowed me some room to play with.

Footwear next; probably the most important bit of my kit for the entire challenge. I had a pair of walking boots and my original plan was to use these as they had served me well climbing Kilimanjaro and any walks I had done since. After talking to many people and seeking advice it seemed that given most of our route would be on national trails or in some cases pavements, boots may be over doing it and walking shoes may be more appropriate. Shoes are lighter than boots and given we would be walking upwards of 20 miles a day this could make a big difference. I sought some good quality walking shoes. I wanted to get these as soon as possible to give myself chance to 'wear them in' however, this was going to be easier said than done. Finding shoes that are comfortable on my feet can be a nightmare; my heels blister easily and if I stop wearing a pair of shoes for even a week and then wear them again my feet can blister. Like most of the population I have one foot bigger than the other and the bones in the back of each heel protrude quite a lot. I knew finding the right pair of walking shoes would be both a nightmare and a lengthy process.

I visited every different retailer for walking shoes and tried on pretty much all their stock. I found shoes that were comfortable on my heels but the crease at the toes weren't in the right place which would lead to blisters occurring if worn for a long time, and others that were the opposite of that. It began to feel this was going to be an impossible task. I purchased, took home and returned a few different pairs as this gave me the chance to walk around the house in them for a while.

After a few months I finally settled on a pair from Millets. They were comfortable from the moment I put them on and felt very supportive around my ankles. Job done. For the next few days I wore them around the house as much as possible to ensure they felt comfortable before walking outside in them as once I had done this, I wouldn't be able to return them. From this point, and the walk actually starting I wore my shoes as often as possible even if it was just a short walk to the shops.

Socks! I needed to try on and test out numerous types of socks and different combinations of these to ensure I had a several options of set up, after all France was going to be warmer than England and I had to make sure my feet were prepared for this.

I already had most of the remaining equipment necessary for the walk, so I didn't anticipate further significant outlay in monetary terms. The next challenge was to sort out where we could camp during the England leg of our walking journey.

CHAPTER 6: THE FINISHING TOUCHES

I had a vague idea of where we needed to stop each night based upon my original calculations for walking mileage per day however these calculations were approximate, and I didn't want to pre-book and pay for every campsite when I wasn't certain our daily mileage could be achieved. Realistically the chances of us keeping to a set 30-day itinerary were slim given the weather, temperature, changes in terrain, climate and toll on our bodies. I decided to book any hotels through booking.com as these could be cancelled up until only a few days before arrival thus avoiding loss of monies. I contacted relevant campsites to ask if they would allow us to turn up on or around a specific day. Most were very accommodating and those that couldn't offer this flexibility I discarded and found alternative ones. This wasn't a major problem but was a little inconvenient as it meant locating a new campsite and then changing our walking route to enable us to reach it. The English part of the route was starting to come together nicely which just left us France to sort out.

Fast forward to July 2019 and time was quickly disappearing. Me and Phil had got married and time had passed on my mums' treatment, she had completed her chemotherapy had surgery and was going through her last few sessions of radiotherapy which she had started the day after our wedding. I was up north for a major diving competition in Sheffield when my mum sent me through a picture of her ringing 'the bell' at the hospital to signal that she had officially finished her treatment. I felt overwhelmed with emotion a mixture of wanting to burst into tears of relief but also being incredibly happy at the same time. While there would still be a long road to full recovery my mum was well on her way.

Being so close to home so I had arranged to meet with Dean and Rachael to look at the proposed route through France which they had planned. As it currently stood, they had planned for us to do a 36-mile day to start with, which seemed incredibly ambitious so we were meeting to see if we could do anything to make it shorter.

We met at a pub at Hollingworth Lake and began to make plans. All the French maps were laid out onto a table and we began looking at where we could go and where there may possibly be a campsite. After some discussion we agreed that walking 36 miles on day one was too ambitious. Rachael and Dean took the maps away with them to set about planning a walking route now based on walking an average of 20 miles per day.

It was August 2019 before we had finalised our route. We had a definite start date of Saturday 14th September and an end date one month later, on 13th October. Our route through England was split into sections that equated to 3 or 4 consecutive walking days followed by a day of rest however, our journey through France meant 7 solid days of walking. We had much discussion about whether or not to incorporate 'rest days' during our time in France. Whilst the consensus was 'no' I must admit that I was sceptical. With some doubt still in my mind I went with the majority decision. This would leave us with one spare day which I 'tagged' onto our ferry crossing of the English Channel meaning once we arrived in England, we would have two rest days before restarting our walking journey from Poole. This also allowed some contingency planning should anything go wrong with our timings and the ferry crossing itself.

I put together a document for the challenge listing our mileage, stopping points and ascent per day. I knew the Garmin would give us all this information, but I never like to rely too heavily on technology. It was for this reason that I also insisted we carry paper maps with us along the way. Should the Garmin break or lose battery we could find ourselves in the middle of no-where with no idea of where we were.

On paper, the first day of the walk would be the longest at 26 miles (nothing like throwing yourself in at the deep end)! It was going to be a tough start. As a group we recognised this could be a problem. Rachael suggested that when arrived in Brest on the Friday that we walk 6 miles to break the back of the next day, this sounded like a good idea and one we all agreed we should do.

After the 26 mile start the mileage across France would vary from 23 to 19 miles per day this seemed achievable given that most of the walk would be on relatively flat ground. England however would be a completely different terrain including plenty of ascents and descents. Of the 17 planned walking days in England only a handful would see us walking 20 miles or more and given that some would include upwards of 3,000 feet of ascent, this would be no easy feat. The last section of the walk included 2 days where there was no option but to schedule in 23, and 25-mile walking days due to a lack of availability of overnight camping spots. Including a day off before we reached these would allow us to reassess the situation nearer the time and maybe make some adjustment such as using that day to cover extra miles so reducing future mileage, and to then taxi back to the planned camping site. A 25-mile walk on our penultimate day including a 4,000-foot ascent was not something any of us were looking forward to!

So that was it. Job done. Our route was planned. Kit all bought etc.; we were ready to go!

CHAPTER 7: SO IT BEGINS

It was an early start on Friday 13th September as we made our way to Southend Airport at 04.00. There was no real feeling of apprehension as we happily astounded the taxi man by telling him what we were about to do. We proceeded through the airport into departures with little difficulty, surrounded by 'hen' and 'stag' do's we found a table at the pub for some breakfast. There we began to talk about what lay before us and our plans for the day. We had our flight and a hotel booked for that night but apart from that everything was still yet to fall into place. We each ordered as much food as we could individually face as after all we didn't really know when our next meal would be. We then proceeded to boarding. It almost felt like we were jetting off on a holiday, it was the only the fact I was wearing walking shoes and a t-shirt with the words 'Quest for Brest' tagged across the middle that kept bringing me back to reality and that was when a small sense of dread came over me. It was really happening. We were going to walk 500 miles from Brest in France to Halifax in England!

Our flight went smoothly up until the point of landing in France where we were held on the tarmac for over an hour due to a security concern in the airport. As the air stewards informed us of the situation there was quite a murmur from the passengers on the plane. People began to guess what the problem was, with one man shouting out 'well its Friday the 13th so what do you expect?' Everyone began to laugh and carried on their private conversations as though this statement had excused any reason for the delay. Word started coming through that it was left luggage that had caused the situation and people were now being let into the airport so before too long we would be able to 'taxi' into our allotted 'gate'. To pass the time I uploaded a quick 'blog' onto our website and updated social media to announce our arrival; this type of thing was going to be key in keeping people interested in what we were doing and to encourage monetary donations to our allotted charity.

Once we had disembarked, we collected our bags and made our way through the airport to our exit. The real adventure was about to begin!

We were now in France and our only way of getting back to England was a ferry some 150 miles away in St Malo. Our only way to St Malo was by foot. What had we let ourselves in for?

The first thing we needed to do was get to Brest, our starting point. Using a mixture of google translate and limited spoken French enabled us to work out there was a bus direct from the airport into the city, so we joined the queue. Once the bus arrived, we learned there wasn't enough room for the four of us, including our luggage. We naively thought if we waited a short time then another bus would turn up, only to find that they came just once an hour. Even though we had plenty of time left in the day we didn't want to sit around for this length of time. Dean and I walked over to a taxi rank and with our limited spoken French managed to find out that it would cost a total of 20 euros to get into town. Considering the bus would have been 4 euros each (16 in total) this didn't seem too bad. We told Phil and Racheal what we had managed to find out, agreed to make our way into town by taxi, and before we knew it, we were unloading our bags outside a typical European hotel in Brest.

Once 'checked in' we proceeded to our room. The sight of 4 brits each with huge rucksacks squashing into a tiny lift must have been quite a comical sight and even more so as we took it in turns to reverse out of the lift and into our room. We each 'dumped' our bags before heading straight out to find a supermarket. The hotel staff were helpful and told us there was a Lidl not too far away, so we headed in that general direction.

We successfully located the Lidl and wandered around it wondering what we should buy. While nutrition was going to be key, weight had also to be a consideration. Carrying too much weight in food and water could 'kill us off' before we had even got 1 mile down the road. I had a good idea of what to get based on my Mississippi experience, during which I had survived on a combination of bagels and dehydrated meals along with tins of tuna and chicken on the side. However, with this trip we been unable to bring a cooker due to airplane laws and regulations which meant everything would need to be ready to eat. I grabbed a few tins of tuna, some lightweight bruschetta bread, numerous bags of nuts and M&M's (which would make a 'trail mix') alongside some cooked meats. Not exactly a menu fit for a king, but it would have to do. We figured this would get us through the first day of walking and we would reassess from then onwards as to what worked and what didn't. On our walk back to the hotel the heavens opened, and we had to rethink our idea of walking 6 miles to break the back of the next day. Instead we headed back to the hotel to do some 'Challenge' admin (i.e. blogs, social media etc.), had a bite to eat and a much-needed rest. Around 2 hours later the rain stopped, we revised our plans again deciding it was time to start our walk home. We collectively decided to leave our bags at the hotel and just carry snacks and water with us on the basis that it would take us less time to achieve the 6 miles of walking carrying less weight. This would also give us a longer 'rest' before starting walking again the next day. The 6 miles took us around 2 hours of steady walking with a few stops for pictures and way finding, this gave us the opportunity to try out the Garmin and to use some of our technological devices.

Before our arrival we had pictured Brest as a very historic and pretty city, but this didn't seem to be the case. Most of our walk was spent on the side of main roads, in ditches, and meandering between industrial estates. When we finally broke out of the cityscape we were greeted by a large cove and sand filled beach, where a large group of women were trudging up and down in the shallow water; a strange sight but we just assumed it must be some form of exercise class. The beach had a large-roped climbing feature with a summit as high as the bridge we now stood on. Rachael and I decided to head down to have a go at climbing it, this was easier said than done as the rope was slacker than we realised and moved quite easily in the breeze. We eventually made it to the top, posed for some pictures before continuing on.

We were greeted by slightly nicer views as we went over a large bridge spanning the sea to finish our walk just on the outskirts of Brest itself. There was a small singular market stall selling fresh fruit and juice, Rachael bought some of the wares as I began to try and figure out how we could get back to our hotel. As luck would have it that there was a bus stop just around the corner towards the motorway. The bus eventually came, and we made our way back to the hotel. It felt good to have finally started our walking journey and I was pleasantly surprised by how fresh I felt after it. Once back at the hotel I stretched out to try and limit the aches and pains that would no doubt start overnight.

We discussed a start time for the next day whilst eating pizza for tea. In my mind I wanted to be off as early as possible to make use of the day light. I figured walking in the dark in the morning when we were fresh was going to be a lot less taxing than doing so in an evening after having walked 20+ miles. I also knew our first day was likely to be slow as everything would be new and we would be learning what walking pace was realistic, how many breaks we would need etc., I suggested we wake at 6am and set off for the bus as 07.00 giving us around 10 hours of daylight but was overruled as it was deemed that was too early. Instead we would wake at 07.45 and be on the bus for 09.00. I had my doubts about this based on previous experience of undertaking challenges; everything takes longer on the first day.

When I had kayaked the Mississippi, myself and my paddle partner Ken had aimed to be at the source of the river and ready to start our paddle by 10.00 on the first day. We had woken up on time but got to our start point around

30 minutes later than planned. It then took us so long to get our boats off the roof of the car, carry them to the starting point and get ourselves fully prepared to go, that it was already 12.00. We had already lost a vital 2 hours of our first day just from being slow and doing everything for the first time and the consequence of this was not getting to our campsite until night had drawn in. I wanted to avoid making this same mistake again especially in a foreign country where there was no guarantee that the locals would speak English and our command of the French language was not good.

To help ensure a relatively smooth, trouble free set off in the morning, I packed my bag as well as I could and headed off to bed. Deep in the knowledge that this was my last night in comfort for a while.

CHAPTER 8: JUST ONE FOOT INFRONT OF THE OTHER

I was woken abruptly the next morning by Phil who was nudging me and saying we had slept in. Somehow in and amongst eating the pizza and packing the previous night none of us had thought to set an alarm, and it was already 07.45! Dean and Rachael were still asleep, so we woke them up and broke the news, cue a frantic 30 minutes where we all used the bathroom, divided up the day's food into each of our rucksacks, reversed ourselves into the lift and then proceeded to the breakfast room.

Once I was sat down with some breakfast in front of me, I began to realise how my body was aching from the previous day. My hips and knees were quite sore but bearable, strangely the worst pain was in my shoulders and back even though we hadn't walked with our bags. The only thing I could put it down to is having carried my bag on my back through the airport and if this was the case it wasn't a good sign considering what was to come.

Pictures of Brest in all its glory had been used for wall paper in the breakfast room and each of us commented how it looked nothing like any of the areas we had seen so far, perhaps we were just in the wrong place and maybe one day we could come back, explore it more fully, and be able to appreciate it. With breakfast finished we stuffed a few extra pain au chocolates into our bags and headed out to find a bus stop that would take us back to where we had finished walking the previous night. The bus arrived at 10.00 and we finally got to where we had finished our walk the previous night at 11.00.

As I pulled my rucksack onto my shoulders the food and water in it seemed to weigh a ton. I was thankful for my diligence in cutting unnecessary excess weight as without it I don't think I would have been able to put one foot in front of the other. I adjusted all the different straps to get the rucksack as comfortable as possible on my back before setting off and then we finally took our first steps of the day to walk up a slip road. It was now over 2 hours later than we had intended to be off; not a great start!

We were on our way with all our possessions on our back. The real challenge began here. I think this is a good time to say that up until this point in my life I had never walked more than 10 miles in one day. Now you may think this sounds ridiculous and as though I had not planned or prepared myself sufficiently for this challenge, but I know my own body and mind. I also had reasons for not having completed several 20-mile walks previously. The first of these was practicality. Phil and I had got married only 2 months before we set out on this adventure (no this was not our honeymoon). Time to go away and train had been nigh on impossible with most of our time having been taken up with wedding planning and preparations prior to the wedding itself. This was followed by a 2 month incredibly busy period with my job, working over and above my normal hours during competition season, travelling up and down the country with my competition squads, and additionally organising and running summer training camps through the month of August. Phil and I had spent little time together since our wedding, in fact this walk would be the first time we had managed to spend more than 48 continuous hours in each other's company. Secondly, had we found time to take a long weekend out and go and walk 80+ miles over 4 days I simply would not have got on the plane to France. Sometimes naïveté about what you are going to undertake can make it easier to do it. Had I already experienced the pain and exhaustion that we would face I would have found it hard to put myself through it again. Going through it when you have no option but to carry on is the best way to get myself through these physical and mental challenges, and also let's be honest if I was a regular walker people probably wouldn't have deemed this a 'challenge'.

I knew the risks attached with this approach, but nothing is worth doing if it doesn't challenge you in some way. I was aware that most likely I would be the least fit of the 4 of us during this walk; Rachael and Dean are keen cyclists and runners who have completed several triathlons, half marathons and other endurance challenges together, Phil was an ex-elite level sprinter who still kept himself relatively fit whereas I was a diving coach who spends quite a lot of time sat behind a desk doing admin duties with limited regular physical exercise. I had accepted early on that I would probably be bringing up the rear on this walk but also that my fitness would increase dramatically as I went on which would allow me to keep pace with the others and I was up for this challenge. To my way of thinking for me personally it wasn't about completing this challenge in the quickest time or killing myself to do it, it was about trying to complete this physical feat for my Mum and to raise a fantastic amount of money for a great charity. I figured if my Mum could get through chemotherapy, I could push myself through some physical pain to help her.

During the first few hours and miles of the day we stuck to walking by main roads as we made our way through the outskirts of Brest, crossing roundabouts and passing numerous villages before views started to open up into countryside and vast agricultural fields. This was more the France I had imagined, dirt tracks, the sun glaring down on us whilst we walked merrily along at a nice pace towards our end point for the day.

About 4 miles into the day I began to feel my heels rubbing slightly. To avoid any escalation into blisters I stopped to apply some kinesiology tape. This type of tape is most often used for sporting injuries however I had discovered before that it is great for protecting feet from blisters and had brought 3 roles with me, 2 of which I had already chopped into small strips just for these exact moments. I took off my shoes and hobbled over to a nearby mound of dirt to sit and look at my feet. My ankle went from beneath me as it rolled into a ditch. I felt a sudden sense of panic. I focused my attention onto my ankle, could I feel any pain? No need to panic, my foot felt fine, so I busied myself applying tape to each foot. I could also feel a twinge of pain under the ball of each foot, so I put on a few blisters plasters as a precaution.

As we walked on our route took us into woods with very wet undergrowth, including wet leaves. It didn't take long for me to 'stack it' as we headed down a steep slope. We laughed it off, after all I wouldn't be the first or last to do this and what alternative was there? We began to encounter a few ascents and descents so I pulled out my walking poles from my bag; these would help to cushion my knees as we walked. Bad knees on day 1 was not something any of us wanted to encounter.

Having completed 10 miles of walking we pulled off the main route onto a side-track to have some food. It was quiet and trees lined the path providing some shade from the sun. I had brought half a foam sleeping mat with me to use as a general ground sheet for sitting on or placing equipment on when the ground was wet, so I got this out for Phil and me to sit on as we began to eat some food.

I felt good. For the first time ever, I had walked over 10 miles and to top it off I was still in good spirits. I finished my food and began to stretch out my legs and shoulders to help alleviate stiffness. About an hour later we packed up our gear and began to move on, as we hauled our bags up onto our backs, we all let out a small groan in unison. In the short time we had been sat down our muscles had seized up. Collectively we looked like a 'waddle' of penguins as we moved down the path back to the main road! Something made me think this may become a regular sight.

The miles now passed slowly, and I began to feel tired. At about 13 miles my feel felt like they were on fire and I suggested we stop for 10 minutes just so I could get some air to them. I laid on my back and raised my feet into the air hoping that elevating them may help to reduce swelling. Our 10 minutes passed far too quickly, and we were on our way again. There was a general sense of tiredness with aching limbs and we agreed to stop at the next town.

Some 5 miles later we came across the town of Sizun and to our surprise and relief places appeared to be still open. We just about hobbled into the nearest café, dropped onto the nearest set of chairs we could find, and sat there silently, as we tried to work up the energy to order a drink. Dean was the only one of us who still had some energy. He made his way over to the bar to place an order and meanwhile I looked over to Phil and we both gave each other a look that simply said, "what on earth have we undertaken"?

I slowly got up out of my chair, dragged myself over to the bar and ordered a coke; I needed something refreshing. Every step hurt somewhere in my body, mostly my legs but my hips and shoulders were also bruised from carrying my rucksack. I felt as though the smallest breath of wind could have knocked me to the floor. Dean announced that we only had 5 more miles to go until we reached our campsite for the night. This meant approximately another 2 hours of walking based on our current pace of 2.5 miles per hour. Urgh!!!!

My body screamed at me as a I threw my bag onto my shoulders and clipped the hip belt into place. Once outside, I momentarily began to feel a little refreshed although the prospect of another 5 miles did feel somewhat possible. This 'refreshment' lasted all of 30 minutes before my legs began to seize up and each step began to take a lot of effort.

When Dean announced we had 2 more miles to go I was physically at breaking point. My feet felt like lead, every movement made caused my bag to push against the purple bruises which had become visible on my shoulders and hips; I was struggling to put one foot in front of another. I knew I had to try to keep myself moving forwards at whatever cost, I couldn't let this break me so early on, this was now mind over matter and I wasn't going to be defeated!

My pace turned to that of a snail as we turned off the main road and up towards the campsite. A long and steep ascent awaited us. It was the last thing I needed or wanted to do but having seen the signpost for the campsite I put my head down, determined to finish, so I could just see my feet moving and not the distance I had to go. Finally, the moment came, and we turned right into the driveway of the site. A note on the door of the reception told us to find any free pitch and the owners would see us in the morning. All I wanted to do was drop to the floor and stay there let alone erect a tent for the night, but I knew if I let myself stop, I wouldn't move again so I set about pitching our tent.

Phil's feet had taken a battering with multiple blisters now on each foot. I put my foot down (pun intended) telling him to "get off his feet as soon as possible and treat the blisters whilst I sorted out our gear". He went off to find a bucket he could fill with cold water to bathe his feet in. On his return he suggested we all put our legs under the cold water in the shower. He had done this and said it had felt wonderful on his aching calves and limbs.

I managed to pitch our tent despite the aches and pains in my body and then immediately headed towards the showers to test out Phil's 'calf relieving technique'. I forced my now swollen feet out of my shoes, removed my sweat ridden socks and positioned my feet half on and half off the ledge in the shower, giving them a good stretch before letting the water crash onto them. The position quickly became difficult to maintain so instead I simply collapsed down onto the cold floor with my head in my hands letting the freezing water wash all over me. It felt like there was no remedy for the pain I was experiencing, both standing up and sitting down took so much effort that I found myself shivering in the same position for 15 minutes until I finally found the strength within me to move.

As I lay in bed that night, I was haunted by the fact this was only day 1 of the Quest for Brest Challenge! What on earth had we let ourselves in for? How were our bodies going to survive this massive test?

CHAPTER 9: NO PAIN NO GAIN

I woke slowly the next morning trying to figure out where I was and what I was doing. It wasn't long before I was brought crashing back to reality when every tiny movement made sent shooting pains through various parts of my body. I couldn't allow negativity to set in so I told myself it would get easier, and I just had to keep pushing through to get to that point.

Phil woke less enthusiastically than me. We looked at his feet, they were a mess! Multiple blisters were both on and under his heels, they looked incredibly sore and fit to burst. We began a process that would, unknowingly to us at that time, become a regular daily routine for the rest of the trip.

We named this 'Foot inspection followed by A&E in the wild'; the process of surveying the damage, popping the blisters and covering them the best we could, to enable us to continue walking.

'Foot inspection followed by A&E in the wild' now completed it was time to pack up our gear. The only way I was going to motivate myself to first move and second get everything packed away was to be competitive with myself. I set myself the target of being the first of the group to have packed my tent away. This may seem silly and ultra-competitive, but when all you want to do is lay in bed, cocooned in your sleeping bag, and avoid reality at all costs, something has to make you move and this was going to be it for me. It would be my "something" to focus on every morning.

My mission started well as I dropped our tent in no time at all and it was packed away before Dean or Rachael had even got out of their tent. Next it was time to pack my bag. I was still a bit of a novice regarding how best to pack everything so I swapped a few bits around from the previous day to see if it would help distribute the weight better. After that it was time to really assess the damage to my body.

I walked over to the shower block. Oh, my goodness, what pain! For anyone who has ever suffered DOMS (delayed onset of muscle soreness) from training or doing sport, times that pain by thousands and it may feel something like what I felt that morning. I felt like my body had frozen overnight, to that of a statue as I coaxed my legs to move one after another. It was at this point that I suddenly became aware of a sharp shooting pain on the top right-hand side of my right foot. I tried to shake it off and simply thought it was just a 'niggle' instead focusing on getting my body moving again. I stretched my body, trying to free up my limbs to get some 'life' into them, before waddling back to our 'pitch' putting the pain in my ankle to the back of my mind.

Not a word was spoken as we hauled up our bags and slung them onto our bruised shoulders and hips. I just kept telling myself that it would get easier, that my body would adapt to this extreme activity and that given we walked 21 miles yesterday the 15 miles we had to do that day would be okay.

Just before we left we met the campsite owners Andrew and Belinda (who just so happened to be British) who advised us that the town of Commana was only 5 miles away and if we made it there before 12.00 (it's closing time) we may be able to get some fresh food. Excellent news! However, it was already 10.00 meaning we would have to 'hot-foot it up there' if we were to stand any chance of the shops still being open.

On that note it was time, and off we went, 4 adventurers on the trip of a lifetime, but …… in the wrong direction. A great start to the day!

Having walked a few unnecessary metres, we now turned around to head back up the road to the campsite to restart our day's journey. After a few mile's, my limbs started to free up slightly, but I was still very much aware of the pain in my foot. A mile or so in I stopped to loosen off my shoe in the hope this may ease the situation, but it made no difference as with each step I took the pain started to creep up my calves and into my quads. I continued walking with a slight hobble, trying to alleviate the pressure on my right foot, but it was no good. I suddenly came to a stop and burst into tears. Tears of pain yes, but mostly out of frustration! I hadn't even managed to walk 2 miles on day 2 and already my body was giving up on me. Phil was by my side instantly and offered to take my rucksack to see if that made a difference but with his feet still causing him excruciating pain, I didn't want him to carry extra weight as this would only add to his own personal struggles. Instead I wiped my tears, dug deep and with renewed determination set off walking again to reach the town of Commana where I could then reassess my situation.

Every step I took, my foot felt as though it was being pierced with a needle. I couldn't understand what had happened, how had I done this to myself? A few minutes later I recalled the incident of having 'rolled over' on my ankle the day before. That must be it, I thought, I've gone and done something to my ankle. Great work Grace! On day 1 of a 500-mile walk trust me to have injured myself to the point of not being able to walk properly.

It seemed to take a lifetime to get to Commana but by some miracle we got there at 11.45 to find the shops were still open. I dropped onto the seats outside and threw my shoes off to get a better look at my ankle. The point of pain on my right foot had now turned purple and was incredibly tender to touch, the position of the pain made me wonder if it was something worse than just a rolled ankle as it seemed to be directly on one of the small bones in my foot and was agony to put pressure on. I just sat with my head in my hands trying to work out how I could possibly carry on the day like this, Phil took one look at my foot and my face then squeezed me tight.

Phil, Dean and Rachael then went into the shop to try and get some food. On their return they told me I had to stop walking, we would source a taxi to take myself and Phil back to the site we had just left, and Rachael and Dean would continue so the miles could at least be covered. I knew it was the right decision, but it still cut me deep. I didn't want to stop, I felt like a failure only having made it through one day, but I was worried that I may have done major damage to my foot. I knew carrying on would be reckless, instead a day of rest may help, after all I still had a month of walking to do. if I pushed too hard now maybe I would have to pull out full stop and that wasn't something I was willing to risk. What was 10 miles over the chance to complete the remaining 464. I felt event worse when I heard Dean say to Rachael that they would now be able to go faster if Phil and I weren't with them. Whilst I understood his point it did hurt me to hear it said.

Now we had to somehow find a way to get back to the campsite. In England it would be as simple as ordering a taxi via your phone. In rural France though it wasn't going to be as easy as that and for several reasons; 1 we didn't speak fluent French, 2 we had little phone signal and 3 we didn't know if you could hire a taxi in this particular area. Rachael used her best 'A level French' to explain what had happened to a shop owner and before we knew it we were surrounded by locals all trying their best to translate back and forth from French to English and we eventually realised there were no taxis running on a Sunday.

It never ceases to amaze me the generosity of strangers when someone is in need as one after another the town's people came over to us trying to help us in any way they could. Soon a small group moved towards us and we recognised their distinctive British accent. One of the locals, hearing of our struggles had walked to the other end of town to get his British neighbour's to come along and help. They explained taxis and public transport didn't really exist in these parts of France, but that one of the locals had volunteered her husband to drive Phil and I back to the campsite. We aren't sure how much of a say this 'volunteer' had in the matter. However, a few minutes later a mature French gentleman pulled up in his car and signaled to us that he was going to take us back to the site.

The English couple confirmed this, so we gratefully loaded our bags into the boot of his car.

The drive back to the site took around 15 minutes. Given it had taken us hours to walk to the town this was quite remarkable. During the short journey we attempted to make conversation with this kind gentleman. I must admit we all laughed as we struggled to understand each other as each of us had limited verbal ability when speaking the others language.

Before we knew it, we were back at the site. We were climbing out of the car when we were approached by a couple who thought our driver was the owner of the campsite. We were shocked when they spoke, they were English! We struck up a conversation with them and discovered their names were Jane and Shaun, they were on holiday and were travelling across France in their campervan. We went on to explain why we were in France, and what had happened to my foot. They were incredibly kind to us as they explained they were going out for the day and if they passed a supermarket they would call in and bring us some food back (we had explained that we had been going to pick up food supplies as we walked along our set route). We exchanged phone numbers and bid them farewell for the day.

About 20 minutes later the owners of the campsite returned from their morning trip looking rather perplexed when they saw us. We explained our situation and politely asked if there was a possibility of us camping for a second night or alternatively asked if they knew how it was possible for us to make our way (other than walking, which was an impossibility) to the campsite Rachael and Dean were heading for. They told us not to worry, we could pitch our tents anywhere we wanted, and they offered to drive us to the second campsite later in the day once they had completed numerous jobs around the site. We didn't mind waiting as this sounded too good to be true! We located a spot where we could set up our tarpaulin, instead of our tent. I'd bought this in case of inclement weather as it would provide shelter in addition to being able to pitch our tents underneath it and would help to keep things dry. In all honesty I hadn't expected to be using it as early as on the second day in France!

With our limited movement it took us a while to decide on the best way to pitch the tarp, but we eventually settled on attaching guy ropes to my walking poles, draping the tarpaulin over these and then pegging them down. I threw all the bags onto the floor, climbed under the tarpaulin and proceed to take my shoes off. To my alarm my damaged foot was turning more purple! A few moments later I felt a sudden sense of tiredness wash over me, so I laid out any sleeping mats we had, curled up on these and fell asleep.

I woke with a sudden sense of alarm as I recalled where we were and why. I checked my phone to see if there were any message from Dean or Rachael, no there wasn't, so I dropped them a message to see how they were getting on. They replied later by sending a picture of them eating ice lollies and ice cream, captioned 'struggling on Grace'. While I'm sure it wasn't meant in that way, it did feel like a slight dig at us; as though everything was much easier and more enjoyable if we weren't there. I tried to shrug it off as me just feeling down and annoyed at the situation we found ourselves in.

The day passed slowly but eventually it was time to head over to our next campsite, so we collapsed our tarpaulin and put all our baggage into Andrews car. Approximately 5 minutes later we were on our way, on the same roads we had only been walking on some 8 hours earlier. We struck up a conversation with Andrew who told us he and his wife had moved out to Brittany many years ago and taken over the campsite. They loved their new way of life as it was much more relaxed and a slower pace than back in England. They explained we had chosen the correct weekend to visit them as the following week they would be fully booked out by a group who came every year and took over the entire site. As we drove on Andrew pointed out places of interest including an Irish pub in one of the local towns (it seems everywhere really does have one) which was one of his favourites. He would have highly recommended it had we had time to call in.

After around 20 minutes of driving our scenery changed and became tall trees and winding roads with steep ascents. All I could think about was Dean and Rachael having to climb these on foot. Ergh!

We turned off the road and headed down towards a stream where our next campsite was located. It was a lovely set up; a long stretch of grass for pitching your tents with trees and bushes sectioning off areas to give privacy. We said goodbye and a big thank you to Andrew, checked in and started pitching our tent. I hobbled around barefooted trying to make myself as useful as possible, with no shoes on I could at least put a bit of pressure on my foot, so we had our tent up in no time. As much as we wanted to sit down and relax we decided to utilise the remaining daylight to set up our beds properly rather than wait until it was dark and then perform movements that can only be described as contortions to both get our beds set up and get ready for bed in a tiny 2 man tent or more realistically one fit for 1 man and his bag.

It wasn't long before we caught sight of Dean and Rachael coming down the road towards us, we hobbled over to meet them and asked how their day had gone. They had 'coped' okay, but there had been a lot of climbing and they were nursing several ailments between them. It became apparent there was now a definite sense of 'what have we let ourselves in for' being felt by each of us.

Once Dean and Rachael had settled themselves down, we started discussing our current food situation, none of us had much left or managed to find a supermarket/local corner shop to stock up other than the one this morning that had supplied fresh food. We had a look in the shop on site but most of the food they stocked required some form of cooking which we couldn't do due to the absence of cooking equipment (as mentioned before this was due to restrictions imposed by the airline, not from any choice of ours). However, there was a tub of Nutella, although not ideal as it would be heavy to carry Phil did have some bruschetta's and bread left that we could spread this onto, so it was our only option.

Having been on route 2 days availability of food was turning out to be a problem that we hadn't anticipated. Our routes were incredibly rural and if we ever did manage to walk through a town all the shops seemed to be closed. The irony of this situation was not lost on me, before we had set off, I had bought many packs of 'Compeed' blisters plasters. We were quickly running out of these and struggled to stock up on these as well. In total I had packed over 25 of these plasters aiming to have enough to get myself and Phil (if not all of us) through France based on each one giving 5 days coverage. We had thought taking more than this was going slightly overboard, however 2 days in and we only had 3 left. Hopefully, this will give you, the reader, some idea of the current condition of our feet. I already had a couple of these blister plasters on each ankle, (these being the usual places I get blisters) and a few under my right foot where I had felt my shoes rubbing on the ball of my foot between my big and inner toe. In comparison Phil was physically walking on 'Compeed'. His feet were enveloped in plaster and tape and showed no sign of getting better. Finding a shop where we could buy a supply of blister plasters and food was now a priority.

I bravely suggested a slightly earlier start to the next day thus allowing more time to complete the walking mileage as if my foot was still very tender, I would be walking slower than anticipated. This suggestion went down like a lead balloon but determinedly I pushed my point and we agreed to set off around 30 minutes earlier! This wasn't exactly what I had hoped for, but this walk did start out as team challenge, so I went with the democratic decision.

CHAPTER 10: HOLDING IT TOGETHER

The following day Phil and I woke relatively early, so we set our tent down and organised ourselves for the day ahead. My foot was aching slightly, and I was aware of it, but with my trainers on I could walk with minimal pain so that was some improvement. Phil was not doing quite so well, having woken up with severe stomach-ache and had spent the morning rushing to and from the toilets. I made a mental note to try and find some electrolyte tablets to put into his drinks to replenish some of the nutrients he had already lost.

We ate bread with Nutella for breakfast before packing our bags and making ready to go. I taped some fabric to my foot where the stabbing pains were in the hope it may cushion my foot slightly and release the pressure from my shoes. It was time for the moment of truth as I switched over from my trainers into my walking shoes. I quickly realised (even before I tied them up) there was no way I could use these for walking in today. Each step was causing the same shooting pains as experienced the day before. Well there was only one thing for it, I was going to have to walk the next 21 miles in my £19.99 lime green Nike trainers. If my Duke of Edinburgh leaders could have seen me at this point, (I remember them telling us very clearly how walking in anything other than walking boots for a long hike was pretty much suicide for your feet), they would have sent me home. I recalled some people had turned up in trainers for their practice walk and they were told they couldn't participate. That was all well and good then but at this point I didn't really have an alternative available other than not to walk and miss another day. I knew immediately which option I would be taking.

I knew given my footwear situation, and the lack of any type of shock absorption provided by the soles, that there was a good chance I would start to feel pain in my knees and hips as the day went on but I needed to keep going so I dug out my walking poles and we set off. It was a long winding climb for most of the morning down the side of a main road lined with trees with not much to look at, so we decided to keep ourselves busy by playing games. First up was the 'Alphabet game'. A game where you chose a specific topic and then take turns to name something from that using a certain letter of the alphabet. If you repeat what someone has already said then you are 'out' of the game, for example the category is sport and the letter is 's' so you could say swimming. This certainly helped to pass time as the topics got harder and required more thought. To this day none of us can think of a vegetable beginning with 'x'.

Considering my difficult start to the day I was feeling good, the sun started to rise and created a pleasant temperature in which we could wander along comfortably. About 5 miles into the day we saw what looked like a town on the horizon. We approached enthusiastically hoping we could stock up on food and medical supplies. As we approached, the town appeared empty and are hopes began to slowly drain away. We were wandering up and down the streets trying to find any source of life when we stumbled upon a town square with a beautiful old church in its centre. Having made good time thus far we decided to have a short break, apply sun cream and have a bit of a snacks. Our spirits were high as we indulged in a eating small amount of sweets and biscuits. We talked about how we all wanted to move to France, after all it was a Monday morning and everywhere still seemed to be closed! We'd understood when we found shops were closed on a Sunday but had assumed places would reopen for business during the week. How wrong we were.

It was time to make a move, so we left our rest site and resumed our walk. Our path soon turned into a dirt track and continued like this for the next 10 miles. It was pleasant walking with a cool breeze and no traffic to contend with. It was at this point that Phil started mention his feet! Apparently, they had been okay up until when we had stopped earlier in the day but now felt uncomfortable, as though the blisters on his feet had swelled up again. I could tell he was in a great deal of pain; it had become agony for him to walk, even if he wouldn't say so himself, and his pace had dropped significantly.

The dirt track now opened up into a clearing scattered with picnic benches with a large map of the local area. We were in luck! There appeared to be a large town just a mile up the road. There was an elderly couple sat on one of the picnic benches, watching the world go by who kindly confirmed that this was the case. Fortunately for us they were English and were able to tell us of a large supermarket in the center of the town which had been open an hour ago when they were there and even better it had a restaurant.

The prospect of having real food for the first time in days lifted all our spirits and it was only a short walk away (albeit up a hill). We set off in single file, our heads down and each deep in thought. It wasn't long before both Dean and I turned to find we had managed to create a significant walking distance between ourselves, Phil and Rachael. Immediately we turned around and walked back towards each of them with Dean stopping off when we reached Rachael and me carrying on down the hill until I reached Phil whose pace was now extremely slow (crawling speed) and was wincing with every step he took. I immediately gave him some water and offered any words of encouragement I had in me to help him make it up the hill and into the town.

It was extremely painful for him but to his credit he made it before collapsing into a heap on the floor outside the supermarket.

I dragged him up into the shop and into a position of relative comfort before unloading my bag from my back and taking off my shoes, (probably the nicest feeling of the day so far) and then went to the counter to order food. My language skills were to be tested again as I tried to order chicken and chips or in French, 'Poulet et Croustilles'. I had recalled that Poulet meant chicken, so I knew this was probably a safe and potentially easy option to get across to the non-English speaking cashier. As with any food order these days it never seems to be simple and my food order was met with a question which I failed to understand. I repeated my order once again in French and pointed to the chicken to which the cashier nodded and repeated her earlier question, this time with a smile on her face. At least she could see humour in the situation we found ourselves in. She repeated this same question, but this time also tucked her hands under her arm pit and started flapping her arms like a bird. I must have looked confused as she started to laugh whilst pointing to her chest area. I looked at Dean for help, but he was as flabbergasted as I was. Suddenly it dawned on us, she was asking whether we wanted chicken breast or wing. I replied in turn and gestured to my own chest to order 2 lots of the chicken breast. Ah the joys of different languages!

Food had never tasted so good as we tucked into our first meal since arriving in France. No one spoke as we crammed as much into our mouths as we possibly could. Once finished I headed back into the shop to see if there were any gel inserts for my shoes; theses might help soften the blow of constantly pounding the pavement with my feet. They didn't have quite what I needed but I managed to get some soft inserts along with some more snacks and headed to the checkouts.

I suggested to Phil that we have a good look at his feet to see if there was anything, we could do to relieve the pain other than him continuing to take ridiculous amounts of ibuprofen. He removed his socks and shoes which revealed several fresh blisters on the soles of his feet, his toes, and heels. As ever we proceeded to pop them with a safety pin, bleed the liquid out and cover them up again. I was extremely concerned that this was only "papering over the cracks" rather than solving the ongoing problem. Phil, determined to carry on, began to re-tie his shoes and said he would walk through the pain.

As the day had gone on Rachael's feet had deteriorated (I have known Rachael years and she is one tough person who does not "give in" easily) and as we walked through the car park to cross the road, I could tell she was struggling. Our pace was slow, and our collective body language suggested no one really wanted to continue walking. I knew someone needed to address the elephant in the room, so I took a deep breath and spoke up.

"Look guys I really think we need to be discussing whether it's sensible to keep going like this. We are in bits and if we don't stop to treat Phil and Rachael's feet properly, they will end up causing permanent damage. I want to complete this as much as the next person, but I don't think we should be putting our bodies on the line more so than necessary to do it".

Silence followed and you could have heard a pin drop.

Together we came to a halt. I took one look at Phil and knew without him saying anything that he agreed with what I was saying even if it pained him to admit he needed to stop. Rachael put her head down and started to scuff her feet around on the pavement, I sensed that she also knew that we should probably stop. Dean broke the silence saying he wasn't going to stop, that he would carry on even if he was on his own. I was startled by this statement as we had started this as a 'team challenge', not an individual challenge and I told Dean this. A heated discussion followed. When asked for her opinion I heard Rachael mumble that she wanted us all to stick together however she didn't repeat this out loud.

I explained to Dean how I felt about him carrying on and that there was no way I was allowing Phil to take another step without us first getting some appropriate medical supplies to treat his feet. I was fighting back tears as I said this. Every word was cutting me up inside and making me feel like a failure. On day 3 of our challenge we were having to stop again. I had to be sensible though and no amount of pride was going to stop me looking after my husband and one of my closest friends. We stood by the roadside for what must have been another 20 minutes while Rachael decided what she was going to do. I explained how ultimately it was her decision but advised her to think about the long run and damage she could do to herself. After what felt like an eternity Rachael repeated that she wanted us all to stick together and for Dean not to carry on alone. Dean asked Phil and I if he could talk to Rachael alone as he knew she was strong and could get through this. I suggested he say anything he needed to in front of us, after all if he felt like Phil and I weren't "up to it" he may as well say it to my face.

Rachael made the decision to carry on. Whilst I thought this was foolish, I had to respect her decision. As she left us, I asked her to be careful and said no one would have thought any less of her had she decided to stop. We all agreed that Phil and I would get some appropriate medical supplies for his feet before making our way to our next campsite however, as Dean and Rachael headed off in the opposite direction I felt at a complete loss as to how to achieve this.

I needed to take stock of our situation and come up with some form of plan. I walked Phil back across into the supermarket carpark where he sat down propped against a wall. He immediately apologised for 'being a burden.' Straight away I told him to stop talking or thinking like that and just pulled him into a hug, while I tried to think logically.

I pulled out my phone in the hope of finding out about any public transport in the area. My search came up with nothing. How the heck were we going to get ourselves out of this predicament! I did however notice there was a pharmacy up the road; maybe we would be able to get help there regarding Phil's feet. Perhaps there was some "light at the end of the tunnel"!

I set off in the general direction of the Pharmacy ready to have my limited French challenged once again.

On arrival I searched the shelves for any sign of iodine gel. Advice from many people back home suggested this was good for curing and preventing infection of blisters. Unfortunately, I couldn't find any so sought advice. Using the limited spoken French I knew together with a variety of gestures I managed to explain what I needed alongside successfully asking for gauze and micropore tape. I left the pharmacy with increased confidence having negotiated the first obstacle.

Next, how to get to our campsite for the night.

I decided our only option was to try and order a taxi inside the supermarket so that's where I headed. Again no one spoke a word of English at the information desk so once again relied on my limited French and gestures to get my message across. Success, taxi now booked, all we had to do was to wait for it to arrive.

The taxi arrived quickly, we were soon on our way and 40 euros later (ergh) arrived at the campsite. Our friendly taxi driver helped us to unload our bags and then contacted the site owner to tell him we had arrived. On our journey we had taken time to explain to our driver why we were in France. She was somewhat baffled by our current location and why we were so far south. We explained that we were following a route planned by our fellow walkers (i.e. Rachael and Dean) so didn't know much about exactly where we were. Just before she left us, she also told us there was a costal route direct from Brest to St Malo that would have been a lot quicker. Great news that had come a little too late!

We pitched the tents, washed our clothes and showered before laying out all our newly purchased medical supplies and tending to Phil's feet. We had a few hours of daylight left so took our time to carefully pop each blister, apply the iodine oil and cover them loosely with gauze. Phil's feet were now more gauze than skin. I tended to the one blister I had between my big toe and the adjoining one. We then munched on some bread with Nutella and got ourselves ready for bed.

Dean and Rachael had set an approximate arrival time of 20.30. Time was slowly slipping away, and I hadn't heard anything from them. I began to worry, trying several times to phone each of them but with no success. Both phones went through to answer phone. My mind now went into overdrive. Where were they? What had happened to them? Time passed. Sometime later I had an incoming call from Dean, it turned our they were fine and had booked into a bed and breakfast, where they were tucking into a home-made lasagne. Apparently soon after leaving us at the supermarket they had realised they had next to no food or water for the remainder of the day. As night began drawing in, they were struggling. Approximately 2 miles away from our current location they came across a town where there was "Bed and Breakfast" accommodation. They enquired about availability, initially they were turned away by owner however then he had a change of heart and let them stay.

I was so angry at this news, not because they were in a comfortable hotel but that they had foolishly set off with no food or water, especially when we had only earlier been in a supermarket! As you the reader is already aware the fact that they had carried on at all was (in my opinion) silly but to have done it under such circumstances they had was beyond ridiculous. For no good reason they had both put themselves in harm's way I immediately made Dean promise that he would not put himself or any one of us in this position again. Before I 'hung up' we agreed to meet at 08.00 the following morning. Phil could tell I was angry when I got off the phone and let me rant away to him as I told him of my frustration at the whole situation. This made me feel better and we now headed off to bed in readiness for another long day of walking.

CHAPTER 11: THE ENDLESS ROADS

I woke early and suddenly the next morning due to having severe stomach pains. I dressed quickly and rushed out of the tent. I was going back and forth from the toilet block for the rest of the morning, the same can be said of Phil. We both felt terrible with horrendous stomach pains and jet black "number 2's". Whatever we had 'got' was making us feel physically weak. On a more positive note, the blister I had treated with iodine, only yesterday, had now turned rock solid and was no longer painful. I still put 'compeed' plasters on as a precaution before packing up our belongings and waiting for Dean and Rachael to arrive. It was just after 08.00 when we all set off together to try to complete day 4 of our "Quest for Brest" challenge.

Most of the day was spent walking single file on the side of roads (often with no pavement) which meant little interaction and conversation. I was determined to get through the day regardless of how much pain I was in. I was not going to stop short of completing the days walk again unless my life depended on it.

We were making good time for the day as we continued following the roads until we reached our next junction. We arrived at a 'T' junction of what can only be described as French highway! We looked at each other in amazement whilst getting out our phones to see if there was an alternative route we could take. There was nothing in the immediate area, nothing for at least another 2 miles. We had been adhering to the rules of the 'Highway Code' by walking in the direction of the oncoming traffic so vehicles can see you and you can see them. That was fine but now we actually had to cross the highway …oh dear! We each lined up ready to do a mad dash crossing of the dual carriageway when the opportunity arose. Thankfully we didn't have to wait long and arrived safely on the other side of the road.

As we set off up the small banking running parallel with the road, I had a sneaky suspicion we might be breaking the law. This was to be confirmed by the number of people regularly tooting at us. It was an uncomfortable and dangerous walk as the banking was full of holes. It was an accident waiting to happen! However, with little space between the banking and the road it didn't feel safe to walk solely on the road either. As a 'trade-off' I ended up hobbling along, walking with my left foot on the banking and my right foot on the road!

We felt the effects of the traffic speeding by as our bodies were hit by powerful gusts of back draft, particularly when large vehicles passed us by. After enduring this for about an hour Dean managed to locate a side road. We could take this instead and it wouldn't take us too far of course but would get us back to relative safety once (wait for it) … we had crossed the highway again!

We lined up again for the mad dash across the highway. Phil and Dean made it right across the carriageways in one attempt but, Rachael and I only made it to the central reservation. An 'official' looking van pulled up next to us and even though we couldn't fully understand what the driver was saying his actions alone told us we shouldn't be walking there. We did our best to explain we were trying to get across to the small road just up ahead. Surprisingly, he seemed satisfied with our answer and let us go on our way. Finally, back to relative safety we were able to laugh at what we had just done but all agreed we didn't want to have to repeat it.

We needed to find a pharmacy where we could top up our supplies of 'compeed' plasters. Dean and Rachael also hoped to buy some iodine gel having heard how both Phil 's and my feet had benefitted since applying it. For once we were in luck. We passed numerous pharmacy's that were open. I managed to buy some soft insoles for my trainers and collectively we bought up all their supplies of 'compeed' plasters.

We decided to stop for lunch in another town, but once again everything was shut. Out came our reliable supply of snacks, tuna and bruschetta was on the menu, not the greatest meal ever but it did the job and tasted okay. Before leaving Phil re applied iodine and bandaged his feet, a process that took about 45 minutes given how many blisters he had. Each time he had to pop and drain each blister before applying the iodine gel and covering each one with gauze.

We now continued on our way, walking up and down roads and soon my knees and ankles were aching from the repetitive pounding from the pavements. Any time I spotted grass I took the opportunity to walk on it, so my legs and feet had a rest.

Late afternoon Dean announced we were about 2.5 miles away from our pre-arranged stop for the night, an Air B&B. This may sound close but remember to us it meant another hour of walking. We were well and truly into what we began to call the "hell miles". Every single day the last couple of miles were proving to be the toughest in that every muscle in your body ached and felt stiff. You were close to the end but not close enough. You still had an amount of walking to complete. All this caused self-doubt to set in, hence the name "hell miles"!

I wasn't going to let myself get into any form of negative thinking, so I put on my headphones and phoned home to help pass the time.

We finally arrived at our Air B & B but the owner hadn't, so we collapsed with exhaustion outside a restaurant just a few metres away to await his/her arrival. Taking advantage of the outside seating we flung our shoes off, took our bags from ours backs and sprawled across it. Rachael gasped as she removed her socks. Her toes looked incredibly sore and were actually bleeding where her nails had dug into the skin. We took a photograph of them for social media purposes and then began to help her clean them up.

The owner of the house finally arrived, and we made our way slowly up the small hill to the entrance. I say slowly as having been sat for a while all our muscles had ceased up and we resembled a group of stone statues that were learning to walk. Slow, laboured and almost robotic.

Once in the house I forced myself to crawl on my hands and knees up the stairs to our room before collapsing on the bed. My legs and feet were so sore that just taking my weight off them felt wonderful.

Sometime later we towards the restaurant down the road to have some food. We walked through the door and immediately noticed everyone turning to stare at us (just like in the movies when the stranger walks into a local). It quickly became clear we were not welcome there which was further verified when we enquired about food and were told in no uncertain terms that we could not get any, despite the fact that a number of people were sat eating just in front of us. What a welcome!!!

After checking google for any other restaurants in the locality we finally had to abandon the idea and went back to the house where the owner had kindly left some packets of rice for us if we wanted them. We didn't have much to go with the rice other than 2 small packets of chorizo bites, but Phil was prepared to have a go at making us something to eat. Phil made us all a culinary delight of rice and chorizo. I don't know to this day whether it was simply because I was hungry, but it tasted absolutely incredible. It's amazing what you can create with so few ingredients to hand!

Having eaten I managed to find a large bowl which I filled with cold water. I then sat down and put my feet into the bowl to try to reduce some of the swelling before heading for a shower. Phil then massaged my legs and applied lots of deep heat to help relax the muscles and we headed to bed. About 10 minutes later the deep heat really 'kicked in'. My legs felt as though they were on fire. I couldn't tolerate this so somehow got out of bed and stumbled downstairs to the shower where I tried to cool them down. I had used deep heat numerous times before but had never had a reaction like this. I could feel the heat rising up my legs and was worried I could be having an allergic reaction. The cold shower made no difference, so I headed back upstairs to bed to try and sleep it off.

CHAPTER 12: A NEW PERSONAL BEST

We knew the next day was going to be hard as it was going to be our longest so far and also consisted of many steep ascents and descents. The pain I had experienced in my foot on previous days had now stopped so I made the decision to change back to my walking shoes which would give my feet added support. We had all agreed to set off walking at 07.00 as this would give us an extra hour in which to complete the day. Even though the first part of our walk was all uphill we made great time in the morning and came across our first town at around 12.00. To our delight there was a small van selling fresh pizza and although they were getting ready to shut (surprise, surprise!!!) to our delight we did manage to buy a few. Chorizo and rice for tea and pizza for dinner, we hadn't eaten this well in days.

With left over pizza lashed to Dean's rucksack in an Asda 'bag for life' (that Rachael had brought with her as hand luggage on the plane) we once again set off walking. However, we soon stopped again when we spotted an Aldi Supermarket. This was an opportunity we couldn't miss. We had to go in to top up our food supplies before continuing on our way.

As usual our pace slowed slightly in the afternoon; knowing we still had many miles to go this was a tough pill to swallow.

Eighteen miles into our walk and with 5 miles still to go each of us was struggling. The 'hell miles' had hit earlier than usual and when we pulled over for a quick 'loo break' in a field it was a struggle to get going again. For the first time in France I felt cold, so I wrapped myself up in extra clothing. My calves were sore, and my right Achilles heel hurt (yes it was beginning to feel like one problem after another) so I taped it up for extra support before setting off to walk the last 5 miles of the day.

The last 5 miles were to prove a real challenge as we soldiered on, a band of unmotivated adventurers! Rachael's feet were sore, Phil was collecting blisters by the hour, Dean's hip was causing him pain, and my feet actually felt like they were on fire, as though they were being stung by nettles each time I took a step!

After what felt like an eternity we did arrive at our campsite for the night. Rachael and Dean were already in Reception when Phil and I arrived. I found the nearest chair and collapsed into it unable to process what we had just achieved. An incredible 23 miles walked in just over 12 hours! A mixture of pride and pain were the only thoughts going through my head as the owner offered us one of his lodges as an upgrade. Delighted, we took him up on his offer.

After discarding our bags, we each collapsed onto the floor in the lodge, where we sat motionless without any energy to even speak. It seemed as though we sat there for hours, saying nothing. We did manage to inspect our feet; no surprises there! Rachael's were continuing to bleed, Phil had developed even more blisters, Dean also had a few blisters and mine looked to be covered in a heat rash which at least explains the 'nettle sting' feeling. We took turns to shower and put our feet in buckets of cold water before heading off to bed for a well-deserved night's sleep.

CHAPTER 13: TEAMWORK AND THE MIGHTY YELLOW M

I woke very early the next morning and struggled to get back to sleep. My right calf was incredibly tight, so I got up to 'roll it out'. I took out a tennis ball covered in electrical tape that had brought with me to use as a roller. (Rolling the tennis ball on aching/sore muscles helps to break up the tightness within and provides some relief). It felt so good to apply pressure onto my calf to alleviate the tightness and aching.

Before long everyone was up and ready to go. Before going to bed I had washed all my socks to see if a clean pair would minimise the rash that had developed on my feet the previous day. I found a dry pair, put these on and hung the rest on the outside of my rucksack to dry throughout the day.

Not long into our walk we came across a local petrol station with a shop attached so we called in to buy a few snacks for the journey before continuing on our way. Very soon we were once again faced with walking single long busy roadsides and this continued for the whole morning.

Phil was having a particularly bad day of it as his feet were incredibly sore and the blisters weren't healing. He was at the back of our line and I was just in front of him. We were walking slowly as the lorry's and cars came whooshing past. I could tell from Phil's body language that he was in a lot of pain; every step was agony for him as we continued up the relentless concrete roads. It wasn't long before a significant gap had opened up between us and Dean and Rachael. I saw them walking further and further away from us. I called out in an attempt to get their attention but got no response. This didn't really surprise me, the noise from the passing traffic was excruciatingly loud. I also tried ringing them several times (without success) to suggest they slow down or wait for us. Unable to make contact I decided as long as they stayed within view, we would be okay.

We continued on our way however, I quickly realised there was no way we were going to be able to pick up our pace or keep them within our sight. I spoke to Phil and we agreed that if we could just get to the top of the hill then surely we would be able to see them again by which time they should have stopped having realised we weren't with them.

We made slow progress walking up the hill but did make it to the top where we saw the road plummeted straight back down before working its way back up again. We estimated that we could see for at least 1½ miles or more ahead and to our surprise we couldn't see Dean or Rachael.

How had they managed to get so far ahead of us without realising we weren't with them, goodness knows. I was angry, not only had we been completely left behind but in addition all our navigational aids were with Dean and Rachael; Dean had the GPS and Rachael had the maps. So, we didn't know where we were, and we couldn't even see our teammates. This was ridiculous. There were many turnings off the main road, and we had absolutely no idea if we were supposed to take one or any of these. Phil and I concluded (rightly or wrongly) that we must have to continue on the road we were on based on the fact that had Dean and Racheal turned off surely they would have noticed we weren't there once they turned round to let us know we needed to come off the road. This situation broke every single rule for team challenges/adventures, you don't leave your teammates behind whatever the reason (other than an unavoidable emergency) and at all times you should walk at the pace of the slowest person in the team. I knew ranting about this to Phil would make him feel even worse than he already did so I took out my Go Pro camera and recorder and ranted away at that instead.

It was a good hour before we finally caught up with Dean and Rachael. They were sat by the side of the road where it finally flattened out. As I approached and threw my bag to the floor. Silence followed and I could sense they were unsure of what to say, obviously feeling awkward about the situation we had found ourselves in. One of them eventually broke the silence.

"We're sorry Grace, we hadn't realised we had got so far ahead." My anger bated a little. At least I didn't have to explain the reasons for my anger. I simply replied by telling them I appreciated their apology but didn't want a repeat of what had just happened at any point again.

Phil joined us as we rested for about 20 mins at the side of the road. I took this opportunity to tape up my right Achilles which seemed to be getting worse by the minute. My feet had swollen up again and putting my shoes back on was harder work than usual as I forcibly squeezed my feet into them. I swung my rucksack back onto to my back and took my first tentative steps. I felt a small sense of relief on realising the pain in my Achilles had subsided slightly. Some small victory at long last!

We now needed to focus on finding some food. We consulted 'Google' to find there was a McDonalds within 6 miles. Excellent! It may not be the best food but at this point it was equivalent to a 3-course meal at a fancy restaurant, so we headed off in the direction of the distinctive letter 'M'.

After several hours of walking we still hadn't come across the mighty shining yellow 'M'. Exhaustion was taking over as we walked down road after road hoping to see something to lift our spirits. The short relief provided by the tape on my Achilles had now warn off and I needed to stop both physically and mentally.

After what felt like the longest walk ever, we finally saw it in all its glory, the glowing yellow 'M' indicating our stopping point. Hallelujah! Our happiness was to be short lived! We approached the building from the back where a huge brown fence surrounded it. There was no access from the back! My heart sank at the thought of having to walk all the way back down the road we had just come up to try and find a road that led to the front of the building. We sank to the floor in disbelief, we were so near but so far. I sat on the kerb and took my phone out. Would google satellite show any form of snicket that we could get through? I did spot what looked like a gap in the trees between 'Mcdonalds' and the lot next to it. Phil went to have a look and success; we could get through. I could have cried with relief as I hobbled through and then collapsed on a seat outside the shop.

I quickly took my socks and shoes off. My socks were wet with sweat, so I put them in the sun to dry out as much as possible. I wondered if this was part of the cause of my discomfort and heat rash experienced the previous day. I took out my tennis ball and began rolling out and stretching my calves to try and ease the pain I was in. Meanwhile, Phil ordered food for both of us. We 'stuffed our faces' before once more hitting the road.

Powered by the 'McDonalds' we made a fantastic start to the afternoons walk, at one point hitting our personal best average of 3 miles per hour. We were 'flying'. Of course, we couldn't manage to maintain this pace for long and our normal pace resumed as we came across yet another hurdle!

Our planned route had us walking down a single straight road for a number of miles and we were happily doing this when we came to a crossroads with a 'road closed' sign in front of where we needed to go. In England 'road closed' usually refers to vehicles and not pedestrians but we weren't sure if it was the same in France? It soon became clear to us that the closure was due to resurfacing of the road (there was a group of men gathered round a large yellow vehicle that was positioned ready to start pouring tarmac onto the road).

Dean looked at the Garmin to see if there was an alternative route we could take but unless we were willing to go at least 2 miles out of our way to get to it there was nothing we could do other than head down the closed one as fast as we possibly could. Full steam ahead we went down the road. Strangely enough the workmen didn't so much as glance at us, so we assumed we weren't breaking any laws. However, it wasn't long before the large yellow work vehicle was started up and began moving quickly towards us, tarmac flowing out at the back. Great! Unbelievably we were now being chased down a rough road by a giant tarmac making machine.

Thankfully, we made it to the end of the road works without any one of us being flattened. At the end there was a man wearing a 'high vis vest' walking towards us. We expected to be reprimanded, but instead he asked us how we were and where we were going. The look on his face was priceless when we said Halifax, UK. After explaining in a bit more detail, he went on to tell us if we remained on this road that we would be able to walk all the way to Spain! We thanked him for this bit of information but assured him that Spain wasn't quite the direction we were heading for and carried on walking.

Our last 5 miles of the day were through thick forest and on muddy paths, so thick was the forest that my 'spot device' (a tracking device for people to follow our progress back home) stopped sending up a signal. A fact I didn't know until later when we received many messages of concern from friends and family.

It was a nice change of scenery and the peace and quiet was appreciated. We took a break just over 2 miles in for a few snacks and a toilet stop before starting our 'hell miles'. As was the now the norm my body was seizing up, each step I took I felt pain in my hips, calves and knees but, determined to complete the day's walking I just put my head down and kept going. Once we arrived at that evening's campsite, I knew we only had one more day of walking in France to do. We were so close now, all I had to do was to walk for another hour and then I would be able to rest.

Our final 2.5 miles of our walking day turned out to be the slowest. Our walking became laboured and required a lot of effort to just put one foot in front of the other. I struck up a conversation with Dean as we both tried to keep our minds off the walking. Slowly but surely, we made our way to the edge of the town where our campsite was located.

It was after 20.00 when we finally arrived. We had been on the move for 14 hours and it certainly felt like it. I needed all my strength and determination to start pitching out tent rather than collapse onto the grass which was our pitch. Phil would have helped but needed to tend to his blisters. We wasted no time before getting into bed other than first completing our necessary 'foot checks'. These completed it was time to get some sleep! Only 1 more day left to go. Hurray!

CHAPTER 14: IN 'GOD' WE TRUST

I awoke at what was becoming my normal time ... 6.00, went through my morning routine of getting dressed, packing away my sleeping bag and mat, re arranging my rucksack and locating my first aid pack so that I could tend to my feet. I would apply Vaseline between all my toes each morning to help stop blisters forming and replace any blister plasters or tape that had come loose throughout the previous day.

I now had only the one blister on the bottom of my right foot but had multiple 'compeed' plasters on the balls and heels of both feet as a preventative measure as these were prone to blisters. Without any protection on them they were likely to flare up within an hour of starting to walk. One major negative of using 'compeed' plasters is they leave a sticky residue on your socks. To try to prevent this, I was sticking Kinesiology tape (the type I was using to minimise the pain in my Achilles) over the top of the 'compeed' plasters. The tape was also helpful in preventing blisters occurring so collectively, we were using small pieces to wrap around our toes. This worked well unless the tape came loose (which it often did) and needed replacing because at this point you ended up pulling of all the blisters plasters as well. It became a time-consuming daily occurrence to monitor and change all my multiple dressings. I had so many 'compeed' plasters on under my feet that walking with no shoes on at any point now felt bizarre and uneven.

Feet sorted, camp packed away and bags on our backs it was time to set off towards St Malo, a mere 21 miles away.

Our spirits were high for most of the day and initially we made good time. We stopped at a small town about 10 miles in where we found a bakery that was open! We pretty much bought out the shop as at that point we didn't know when we would find any more food. It was incredible value for money, and we were all amazed by the owner's overweight cat being fed bread and sweet food by the minute.

We continued walking at a good pace but were all struggling physically. Eight days of continuous walking was taking its toll on the body. For the first time on the trip the temperature was soring. It was the kind of heat that completely saps your energy on a normal day never mind one where you're carrying over 12kg on your back whilst trying to walk 21 miles. It was because of this we agreed that for every 5 miles completed we would take a 10-minute 'break'. A 'break' is perhaps incorrectly used here. It was more a 10- minute opportunity to air our feet, massage our many ailments, re apply tape and plasters and take our next does of ibuprofen. At this point I was taking 3 500mg tablets every 3 to 4 hours, an excessive amount but, it was the only way I could numb the pain and keep on walking.

As we got nearer to St Malo the roads became much busier and the French drivers frequently tooted their horns at us and other drivers on the road. It made us jokingly question whether walking was within the law France! One situation made us all laugh for a while. Dean and I were slightly ahead of Phil and Rachael, so we stopped to allow them to catch up. As there were no pavements to walk on, we had walk on the roadside. We noticed a car approaching them from behind which pulled up to within a few feet of them. The driver began tooting her horn at Phil and Rachael and continued to follow them, driving extremely slowly. We couldn't comprehend why she didn't simply overtake them given the road was wide enough for two double decker busses to pass each other. She must have been telepathic and finally pulled out passing them on the left whilst shouting what we assume were French expletives out of her car window. Phil simply replied with 'good afternoon, lovely day for a walk' as she zoomed off shaking her head.

In the afternoon we finally began seeing signs for St Malo and the reality that we were going to make it started to hit us. At around 16.00 and with 9 walking miles to go we stopped for one of our '5 miles rests' this time in a field just off a main road. It was going to be a late finish but considering we were going to be staying the night in a hotel rather than a tent, arriving in the dark wasn't going to be a major problem.

It had become part of our routine that any time we stopped Rachael would consult 'google maps' to see if the distance left to walk matched that of the Garmin. There had been a few occasions where 'google' had shown that we had less miles remaining than we originally thought, this was always a good moment, so we nicknamed 'google maps' as 'god'. On this occasion Rachel reported that 'god' indicated we only had 6 miles to go! After a few minutes of us consulting both 'god' and the Garmin we agreed (much to our relief) that we did only have 6 miles to go to reach St Malo. The extra 3 miles on the Garmin led us directly to our hotel on the far side of the city from where we currently sat.

"What do you reckon Grace, where should we class as our finishing point for the day" asked Dean? Our aim had been to walk from Brest to St Malo, and in my mind seeing and even touching the road sign that said welcome to St Malo was going to be good enough for me, failing that reaching the city centre would be more than enough. Either of these options qualified in my opinion and I said so. I seemed to have said what everyone hoped to hear so we took an extra few minutes resting time knowing we now had only 6 miles to do and could probably complete our walk by 18.30.

We decided to use this newfound extra time to call at another McDonalds to get some food to eat. Two McDonalds in as many days felt awful but considering we were burning well over 4000 calories a day we figured we may be okay and might not be too damaging to our health.

We had 4 miles remaining, 4 miles until we had completed this incredible feat that had seemed impossible at so many times.

We took a slightly different route to that advised by Garmin to make sure we avoided another highway incident and instead meandered through a housing estate that ran parallel to the road. We hit a stumbling block when it seemed there was no way back to the road at the other end of the estate. I pulled out my head torch as we headed down a dark path lined with trees in the general direction of the road hoping there would be a way through. The light was fading fast and it was getting hard to even see each other. The path opened into a clearing with another road heading steeply down the side of a large building however, there was a barrier across stating it was government property and trespassers would be prosecuted! We could see the main road at the bottom of the hill approximately 100 metres away. A quick consultation with 'god' told us if we didn't take this route it would be a long walk back up the hill and around the housing estate to get back to the road. Without so much as another word we ducked under the barrier, heading silently and quickly towards the road we needed. We were in stealth mode, unsure of what would happen if we got caught and I switched my head torch off reducing the possibility of us being detected. Visions of being caught by armed guards with flashlights or alternatively setting off sirens and search lights ran through our heads! We gradually picked up our pace to a slight run making it safely to the bottom of the hill. The road veered round to the left where we saw a large open door in the building that could be a loading bay. We came to a sudden halt expecting to be caught or even worse, arrested! We collectively let out a sigh of relief when nothing happened and ran the remaining 50 metres to the main road as fast as our legs would carry us.

Once on the road we could see the lights of St Malo perched high on a cliff; we needed to cross a bridge and we would almost be there. We kept our eyes peeled for a sign saying we were officially in St Malo having agreed that once we saw one, we would stop there.

At first glance it seemed crossing the bridge may be difficult as there wasn't an obvious path for pedestrians. I then remembered from my original planning (when we were going to do the walk the other way around) that there was crossing for pedestrians on the right side of the bridge, as we would have approached it. (I had made a point of checking things like this early on so we knew if we could walk across or needed to get a ferry). This meant the pedestrian crossing I had previously seen on 'google' would now be on the left side of where we were now stood. I spotted what looked like a subway under the road so headed towards it and came out next to a narrow white walkway that ran the full length of the bridge. We paused for a few moments for Rachael to get her head torch on and I reactivated my own. It was now pitch black with the only additional lighting coming from car headlights. Rachael set off at an incredible pace across the bridge to the point that we all struggled to keep up. We finally reached the other side and took some time to catch our breath. Having still not seen a sign saying St Marlo we decided to head towards the centre of the city and call that our finish.

To avoid main roads, we decided to head left off the bridge into a wood that according to the Garmin would wind its way up the cliff face and come out near the main streets of St Marlo. The following miles were horrible, trying to work our way through woodland with very little light, where the ground was extremely uneven was an accident waiting to happen. We all began to flag, as once again we hit our 'hell miles' but this time with the additional difficulties imposed by the woodland. We couldn't see and were relying on pure guess work to get through.

My Achilles was now becoming unbearable! Every step I took I could feel a shooting pain go straight up my calf to the back of my knee and in addition I felt to have very little movement in my ankle. I was hobbling more than walking. All I wanted to do was finish.

We finally broke free of the woods and began to walk down the city streets in a direction that we believed went to St Marlo city centre. We had now walked in excess of the 6 miles we believed that we had left to do, and we were all exhausted. On we went not really having a set end goal other than getting to St Malo. (I noted to myself this had been a big oversight in the planning, and we must learn from it should we ever attempt to do anything like this again.) With every step my pace was slowing and my legs seizing up, I had never experienced anything like, it was as though my body was completely shutting down and refusing to let me carry on.

I tried to distract myself from the pain by taking in my surroundings, looking for anything that could signal a stopping point or somewhere we could get a taxi to our hotel. I saw a sign for an Ibis hotel with an arrow pointing in the direction we were going and the number 0.8, surely this meant there was an Ibis less than 1 mile away from us. I shouted to the others to suggest we stop there and ask the receptionist to ring for a taxi for us, we had walked more than enough for that day., We were well and truly in St Malo and walking trying to find a sign to say so late in the day when we were all in such pain seemed ridiculous. Everyone agreed.

Now I just had to get myself to the Ibis 1 mile down the road but I just stood there on the pavement in agony trying to hold back tears, I tried to tell myself we had less than 1 mile to go and I could do this even if I had to hobble to get there. I tried to stretch out my legs before curling into a ball with my head in my hands trying to get a grip of myself and what I had left to do. It was only 1 more mile, 1 more mile of pain and agony but only 1 more mile, but the tears began to fall. I just stayed their motionless. My body was done, and I couldn't move without pain firing through my legs. I soon felt Phil grab my arm and lift me to my feet saying.

"You can do this, just hold on to me, we will do it together." I wiped away my tears, wrapped my arm around his shoulder to take as much weight as possible off my right leg. I pulled out one of my walking poles into my left hand to try to use this as some form of support and we began to slowly move forwards, Phil walking and me hopping whilst pulling my right leg along behind.

That was probably the slowest mile of our whole week as made our way down the road towards the lit-up Ibis sign. Only 0.8 miles way.

I don't know how we made it to the hotel entrance, but we did. Phil lowered me down onto a chair and I sat there exhausted in complete awe of what we had just achieved. From day one my first goal had been to make it to St Malo, I wasn't thinking about the rest of the walk (that was another challenge altogether and for another day) we had done it, we had walked to St Malo! I then threw my shoes off, laid down on the floor, raised my feet into the air to try and get rid of the throbbing feeling in my feet and put my hands over my eyes. WE HAD DONE IT!

In a taxi ordered by the Ibis receptionist we finally arrived at our accommodation. I sat in the shower not able to hold my own body weight anymore and began to remove all the tape, plasters and 'compeed' that had quite literally been holding me together for the last 8 days. For the first time in that 8 days I could actually stand on my feet properly (albeit with difficulty) without mounds of 'compeed' all over them.

We went to bed that night with a feeling of relief knowing we didn't have to walk multiple miles the next day.

Our ferry was just after 10.00 the next morning. We arrived early and got a bite to eat before boarding. Once on board we headed to the top deck to watch France fade away from view as we steamed away. We kept getting a number of looks from other passengers (after all we were in our matching 'Quest for Brest' tops, and none of us was able to walk without some form of limp) and a number of them asked what we were doing. We got quite a number of monetary donations from people on board which were gratefully received. These mixed in with some donations from generous French citizens meant we had around £200 in our tin before setting foot back in England.

The first match of the rugby world cup happened to be showing on the big screen in the bar so we sat to watch, after all the journey was going to take 8 hours and we planned on spending as much of that time relaxing and keeping off our feet at much as possible.

We arrived in Portsmouth on schedule and waited until we were told to leave the ferry. Allen a friend and work colleague of mine had offered to drive from Southend to pick us up from the port and take us across to Poole where we would be continuing our walk up to Halifax. (Our original plan was to cross from St Malo to Poole but the cost of this and the timings of the ferries made Portsmouth a much more viable option) It was great to see a friendly face and we chatted away happily about our journey and asked how everything was back at home.

Once in Poole we headed to our accommodation for the night, luxury, a static caravan that had enough beds for all of us and was fully equipped with a much-needed washing machine. We then headed out for some pub food. Thankfully England is not like France in this respect and restaurants are actually open during the day.

At the end of our meal I was shocked to see my Mum and Phil's Mum/my mother in law (Jackie) walk around the corner to meet us. Apparently, this had been planned last minute with Allen and without our knowledge. It was a great surprise and I hobbled over to give my Mum a big hug, she looked well, and it was amazing to see her.

CHAPTER 15: HOME IS WHERE THE 'START' IS

Waking up the next morning knowing we had a day off was wonderful, but we had lots to do and no time to rest. The quicker we got things done the more 'down time' we could have. I did the normal routine of checking and treating my feet as needed and we headed out into Poole to find a 'Go Outdoors' and places where we could stock up on food.

Given our walk was now going to be in England and an autumnal England at that we needed to make sure our clothing was 'British weather-proof'. We had carried little in terms of major waterproofs or thick layers through France due to the warmer climate and the need to cut back on weight so a trip to the shops was a must to get a few extra layers.

I had pre planned this eventuality and Allen had brought with him (from Southend) a large bag containing warmer clothes, my hiking boots, my 1-man tent and all the maps for England amongst many other things. However, the weather forecast for the next week was showing continuous showers, so I planned on getting an extra cheap top and a thin long-sleeved layer as a back-up if we got wet through.

We spent hours in Go Outdoors stocking up on clothes, new camel packs, and a completely new stock of walking socks (my original 3 pairs from France we in bits due to the blisters plasters that I had been wearing). Rachael wanted to find some new shoes to wear due to the problems she had had with her feet in France. Her feet had swollen to such a point that she could no longer fit in her shoes. Instead being a keen runner, she was looking for some fell running type shoes that she knew would be comfortable to wear.

Food and clothes sorted we headed back to the van to wash all our clothes and sort out our gear. I repacked my back to include my now 1-man tent. Phil would be leaving the journey at this point to return to Southend with Allen, due to work commitments, so I now had to transfer any gear he had carried for us both into my bag. It took quite a bit of rearranging and I discarded a few things I hadn't yet used to save weight. Once sorted I now had to make a crucial decision. Since changing out of my walking shoes I had not had as much pain in my Achilles and I was beginning to wonder if the tightness of the shoes due to the swelling of my feet was the cause. I iced my feet that night to try and bring the swelling down as I debated whether to carry on in the walking shoes or switch over to my walking boots that Allen had brought with him.

I spent some time switching between boots and shoes trying to decide what was best to wear. I knew switching footwear could be a blister risk given that it would be like starting again, but I had worn my walking boots when I climbed Kilimanjaro and for all other walks since and not once had they given me any blisters. I knew from memory they were roomier than the shoes I had been wearing in France.

I made my decision once I squeezed my feet into my walking shoes again. My feet immediately felt tight and not only that I instantly felt the pain in my Achilles. In comparison my walking boots felt breathable and spacious. They caused a bit of pain around the top of my ankle where a lot of the swelling was, however, Phil had a look and tied them up for me just to the top of my foot so they wouldn't press onto my ankles as much. This was the most comfortable I had felt in days and my decision was made. I would change into my walking boots.

Decision made it was time for the moment I had been dreading all day. It was time for Phil, Allen and both Mums to leave and head to their respective homes. I felt sick saying my goodbyes and didn't really know what to do with myself. It felt as though my support network was disappearing and I suddenly felt very alone. I had known this moment was going to be hard, but it still didn't stop me wanting to get in the car and head home with them. Obviously, I didn't do that, I had set myself a challenge and I was determined to complete it.

Having planned the route to include a rest day every 3rd or 4th day I now told myself to take it one bit at a time, to focus on getting to Bath, our first rest day, 4 days and 74 miles away. Even better the 3rd and 4th day were each under 20 miles a day. This was due to how it had worked on the maps along with finding places to stay etc. So, all I had to do was to survive the first two days of 20+ miles and then it would be 'plane sailing', right? Wrong! With the smaller mileage would come bigger hills and even bigger challenges!

Little did I know then what trials and torment we would go through during the next 3 weeks making everything we had faced in France look like some form of all-inclusive luxury holiday.

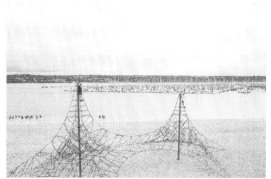

Left: Rachael and me at the top of a climbing frame on the beach in Brest. You can just make out the back end of the exercise class that was going on in the sea to the left.

Right: Rachael looking like she has had enough on the first day, metres away from the hill climb which would lead to our campsite.

Left: In deep thought on the morning of the second day. Phil managed to capture me returning from the toilet block worrying about the pain that had just started in my ankle

Right: Setting out walking again on the morning of day 2

Above: Trying to stay positive in camp on day 3 while waiting for Dean and Rachael to arrive

Above: First aid in the wild. After stopping for the day, I bought supplies to try and treat Phil's blisters. I felt like some form of surgeon

Above: Whenever my Fitbit buzzed to tell me we had walked 10,000 steps we pulled out a bag of M&M's as a celebration. It scares me to wonder how many bags of these we went through

Above: When we had very little food left Phil created this masterpiece. Choritzo and rice, I still dont know if it was just beacuse I was so hungry, but it tasted incredible.

Left: A quick stop off on route was always another chance to check our feet and put on more tape or plasters.

Right: A quick stop on the roadside was an opportunity to stretch out my calves, by this point I was in a lot of pain with my achillies.

Left: Rachael consulting 'god' (google maps) to see just how far we really had left to go.

Right: After our longest day so far, at 23 miles I collapsed in a chair at the campsite. This picture was taken just before we found out we were being upgraded to a 'hut'

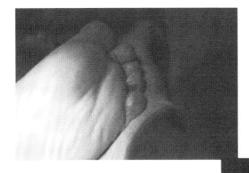

Left: It's safe to say our feet took a battering during the walk, here is a picture taken within the first few days of the underside of Phil's toes.

Right: Collapsing on the floor at the Ibis hotel on arrival into St Malo after having walked 24 miles

Left: Just leaving St Malo on the ferry over to Portsmouth. Wearing our matching T shirts and hobbling around certainly drew some attention.

Right: Arriving into the youth hostel at Cheltenham. I was beyond being ready for a lie down at this point.

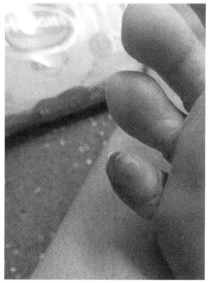

Left: My infected blister, who would have thought something so small could cause so much pain.

Below: Outside the B&B in Blandford Forum with the owner Tania. It was raining heavily so we had layered up before leaving the warmth of Tania's accomodation

Right: My feet after crossing one of the particulaly muddy fields. This shot won the vote on our Instagram story for carrying the most mud.

Top left: Rachaels feet after the 'poogate' fiasco

Top right: Just one of the many signs we came across while preparing to cross another field

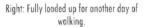

Right: Fully loaded up for another day of walking.

Left: We were joined by friends and family for our final day of walking. It was hard to stay together as a big group but I managed to snap this picture of some of us around the half way mark.

Right: On arrival at the Piece Hall we had to wait a while until the arrival party were ready to receive us. We almost felt like celebrities, surronded by people taking pictures.

Below: The moment finaly arrived as after 28 days of walking we made it to the finish line

Left: We were contacted a few days after finishing by a friendly stranger who had snapped this shot of us arriving at the Piece Hall.

Right: We were welcomed home by family and members of team Macmillan

Below: Once the crowds had dispersed we managed to get a big group shot of all our friends and family who had walked with us or been there to celebrate our big finish.

CHAPTER 16: A CHANGE IN FORTUNE

Knowing the poor weather forecast we got up at 5.00 the next morning aiming to be on our way by 6.00. Torrential rain was due at around 12.00 and we hoped that if we made good time, we could be safely tucked away having some lunch at that point.

Given the increase in equipment I was now carrying my bag was heavier than before and I let out a groan as I threw it on my back. I took some time to rearrange the straps of my rucksack, so it sat on my hips more and now felt almost weightless. Result!

As we walked through the deserted caravan site to the pathway that would take us on our way the sun was still below the horizon. We felt better for having had 2 days off our feet and almost, I say almost, had a spring in our step. My feet felt good in my walking boots and I felt positive about our journey.

We made brilliant time and hit 12 miles out of our 21 before 12.00. One thing we quickly realised was this walk was going to be different to our walk in France. The number of stiles we have in England is ridiculous! That day alone I would not be surprised if we had to go over 40 of them. Stiles can be a difficult at the best of times, but these had metal handrails that come together to form an incredibly narrow gap at the top. Normally you would have to go through these sideways but imagine what it's like with a rucksack on your back, they are a nightmare and near on impossible to negotiate. On top of that it would seem we English love to place a gate between fields, usually one where you push the gate forward, step into the gap, and then push the gate backwards to get through, again impossible to use with a 45 litre rucksack. For every stile or gate, we had to negotiate we probably wasted 5 minutes getting the 3 of us through it. Hilarious to start with but the novelty soon wore off as the days went on.

Our stop for lunch came at the right time as we sat under a wooden shelter in a park to eat our super noodles which we cooked using a jet boil. The heavens opened during our lunch and we were so glad not to be walking in it. Thankfully, it passed quickly, and we were back on our way.

All was going well until about 5 miles away from Blandford Forum when I felt a sudden sharp pain under the heel of my right foot. I took off my shoe to have a look but couldn't see anything stuck in there, so we carried on.

About 2 miles on the heavens opened again and this time there was no shelter to be found so it was waterproofs on and head down. I was still very aware of my foot and the pain was getting worse, I was sure I must have a form of splinter in my heel and stopped to have another look under the cover of a tree. There was nothing visible and as much as I squeezed nothing showed up. All I could do was get to our campsite and have a good look under some light.

With the rain not letting up we made the decision to change our route and to continue on into Blandford Forum itself to see if there was a cheap B&B that were we could get a room, then at least we could dry out our clothes and have a warm shower.

As we changed our direction and headed down the main road to the town my heel was becoming more and more painful, I began to do what I had become accustomed to doing on the walk and began to hobble the rest of the way, trying to minimise the pain as much as possible. On arrival in the town we found a small B&B called St Leonards Farmhouse and knocked on the door to see if they had any rooms. No one answered and then we saw a sign in the window to say there were no vacancies. Not wanting to stand in the rain we remained in the porchway and started using our phones to see if there was anywhere nearby that had rooms.

Call it good luck or fate but moments later the owner of the B&B pulled up in her car. We explained our situation and she let us in to the building to dry off while we searched for somewhere to stay. She was incredibly apologetic that she was unable to accommodate us, and you could see her trying to think of a solution to our problem. She suddenly said she had a double room available. I replied by saying I would happily sleep on the floor if she agreed to me doing so. Her previous look of concern immediately disappeared, and she started smiling. She quickly set to showing us around the place, all the while apologising for not having 3 beds. She felt awful about me having to sleep on the floor. I told her it was fine I had my sleeping mat to keep me comfortable and we were just incredibly grateful for her help.

Showered and with our feet up by 16.00 had to be some form of record for the walk so far. I sat by the window in the room and had a good look at my foot, there was defiantly nothing in there and it was starting to look more like I had large blister that had yet to come through fully. I was relieved that I now knew what the pain was and could perhaps do something about it. I set about doing the treatment process we had followed in France for blisters, but nothing would come out of this one, it was clearly too deep under the skin. I prayed that by some miracle it would come through overnight and I would be able to pop it in the morning so I could at least walk a bit easier. Ha, ha, ha, a nice thought!

Tania the owner of the B&B came to our room a few hours later to tell us someone hadn't turned up for their single room so if I wanted I could have it free of charge. Obviously, I said yes, packed all my things and moved across the hallway to an immaculate single room with one of the most comfortable beds I have ever slept on. I was so grateful to her.

CHAPTER 17: THERE IS NO I IN TEAM

I awoke early next morning and got out of bed to assess the foot situation. I tried putting my foot down. It was not good. If the day before had been bad this was horrendous! I was unable to put any pressure on my heel without feeling as though I was being stabbed by a needle. I spent a good hour using mole skin (a durable material that is good for protecting against blisters, especially on the feet) to try and find a way to ease the pain. I cut a number of small squares and then in each cut out a circle in the middle about the size of my blister and began sticking them one at a time to my foot with the aim of creating a pad of fabric that would ensure the blisters itself didn't touch the insole of my shoe. I headed down to breakfast with my feet looking like a badly put together patchwork quilt!

Tania put on quite a spread for our breakfast, including bowls of fruit, cereal and all varieties of cooked food. It was good to finally be getting a decent amount of food before a full day of walking.

We got to talking to a fellow guest who was asking what we were doing. She was shocked and thought we were mad especially once we told her the rain had not stopped falling all morning. Her reaction was understandable and none of us felt particularly motivated to get going.

Having earlier decided we would wait a while to see if the rain abated, we had to make the decision to simply bite the bullet and get going as it was already 10.00 and we still had 20+ miles to walk that day. I quickly checked my feet again, applied Vaseline between my toes and on any suspicious blister areas (this helps to stop blisters developing) and set to putting my socks and shoes on. It was time to try and stand up and see if my blister contraption was going to work. Unfortunately for me it didn't and as soon as I put weight on my feet the sharp needle like pain came straight back. I knew there and then that walking was going to be hard.

We assembled downstairs were Tania was waiting for us. As we layered up and put on our ponchos, she looked at us in disbelief that we were about to go out in the weather. She offered us another night's stay in an attempt to stop us. Having seen my feet at breakfast she asked how I intended to walk. I told her I had no option but to just keep going, I had a challenge to complete although I must admit we all stood there reluctant to open the door and go. We finally said our goodbyes and thank you's then stepped out into the downpour.

Thankfully as the morning went on the weather cleared up. The route now included climbing, as soon as we reached the top of one hill it would be straight back down the other side and then back up again, it was tiring work and extremely hard on my feet. The only way I could keep going was to walk on the outside of my foot or on my toes, but this meant I wasn't able to move particularly fast and we only managed 7 miles in the time we would usually hit about 12. At this pace we wouldn't make our campsite for the night until the early hours of the morning.

We rested at the top of one of the accents and I took the opportunity to remove my shoes and ease the pain on my feet for a few minutes, it felt wonderful. Putting the shoes back on however did not. Up and down we went all day with me hobbling along at the back.

At the top of one of the hills clouds rolled in incredibly fast and we got caught in a tremendous thunderstorm. We attempted to get down as quickly as possible but were met by a scattering of cows and then just to the left a giant bull. Wonderful. Stealth mode on we calmly made our way past the bull and to the safety of the path beyond the gate at the bottom of the hill. On our decent we had been able to see a path that rose (once again) steeply up. From our perspective it may as well have been vertical. I heard Rachael let out a groan, asking if we had to go up that. I prayed that we didn't, the pain in my feet wasn't letting off and I was in agony. It was in vain. Yes, we were going up that!

I stood at the bottom of the hill looking up at this huge climb standing before me, with no blisters or rucksack this would have been a difficult climb never mind in my current situation. I took a deep breath put my head down and set to.

It wasn't long before I needed to use my hands to help me move forward. Only being able to walk on the toes of my right foot was making progress difficult as I wasn't getting much power or stability from my feet as I climbed, so I was now on all fours slowing pulling my way up the hill. Dean had already ploughed his way to the summit and was coming running back down having dumped his gear at the top, he came shooting past me to Rachael offering to carry her bag the remainder of the way, but she was determined to do this on her own and turned down his offer so he ran back up the hill!

I took a deep breath, a swig of my drink and rearranged my rucksack, I was about halfway, all I needed to do was get to the top where I could rest for a while. Head down I carried on.

Finally, after what felt another summit attempt of Kilimanjaro, I made it to the top. Rachael was close behind me and we all took a short break to catch our breath. It was at this moment that I realised I was quickly running out of water, I had gone through my camel pack and was now onto the last remaining dregs of my bottle, not ideal at all. I took a conservative gulp of my water before carrying on.

We were now 10 miles away from our campsite and it was already 16.30, even at a good pace we wouldn't make it there until 20.30 and to top it off we still hadn't eaten.

Shaftsbury was 5 miles away, so we settled on making it there and finding some food to eat, before carrying on to our campsite. My heart sank, 5 miles that was at least another 2 hours of hobbling in pain and discomfort. We were now walking alongside roads again so I decided to change into my trainers given that it was no longer muddy, and they may offer some relief to my foot. I had a quick look at the blister that I had covered in the morning to see that it had now spread round to my ankle. Fortunately, it was no longer under my skin but instead had formed into a giant bubble which meant one thing, I could at least pop it. I got out my safety pin and hand sanitizer and set about performing a roadside blister popping operation before covering it all up again and lacing up my trainers.

While my foot still hurt, switching into my trainers had been a great idea, hobbling along in trainers that weighed little was much less of an effort than hobbling along in walking boots. We eventually made it to Shaftesbury arriving just after 18.00. I felt a sense of relief and pride, even in all that pain, with every fibre of my body urging me to stop, I had successfully completed 16 miles.

We found a local pub and ordered ourselves drinks and a plateful of food each. While waiting for our food to come one of the locals struck up a conversation with us, after asking what we were doing he began telling us about the history of Shaftsbury and how there was a street just down the road called 'gold hill'. This street was the one made famous by the original advert for Hovis Bread. Dean and Rachael both wanted to go and run up it. I would have joined them given any other situation but as much as I wanted to join them, I knew with my foot that I couldn't so remained in the pub resting my feet.

On their return we ate quickly, we still had 5 miles to go and it was nearly 19.00 so we had no time to waste. We had about 45 minutes of sun light but about 2 hours of walking left to go and on arrival we still had to pitch our tents. Our route was now along country roads with no paths and we would soon be walking in darkness. It was turning into an almost impossible situation.

I knew what I should do so I spoke up.

"You two go, I will take your bags, get a lift to the campsite and pitch the tents before the sun goes down"

I knew I was the reason our pace had been so slow throughout the day. I had managed to hobble 16 miles and I was proud to have made it to that point, but I knew if I tried to carry on, I would put everyone in unnecessary danger. To my surprise Dean and Rachael didn't agree to my suggestion straight away suggesting instead that we try and find somewhere to stay in the town and simply add another 5 miles to tomorrows walk. I was conscious of the extra expenditure. We were on a tight budget in terms of accommodation and we had already booked our campsite. Alongside this adding 5 miles to tomorrows walk would mean another 20+ mile day as opposed to the planned 16. I had managed to do 16 miles that day, yes it had been a slow pace, but we had done it meaning even if my foot didn't feel better the next day there was a good chance I could at least hobble along and still complete the miles. Adding another 5 miles would make it impossible to achieve it within daylight. I didn't know how long my feet would take to recover and I didn't want us to get to a point where we were having to drop miles each day making our end task impossible within the time frame we had allowed. We talked it through and decided to go with my idea.

I'm not too proud to know when to 'take one for the team'. Yes, it would mean missing a few more miles but in doing so I could at least allow Rachael and Dean to finish the day properly and safely whilst I set up the tents ready for their arrival. My role was simply switching from walker to support crew for a couple of hours and I was fine with that, even if I did feel a sense of disappointment within myself. So, the plan was set. I would go ahead get my tent set up and sort my blisters out and then if possible, would pitch Dean and Rachael's tent as well.

We ordered a taxi for me. Dean and Rachael waited until it arrived and then set off. It was a 30-minute journey by car to the site during which the driver was incredibly chatty. I explained about our 'Quest for Brest' Challenge and why I was not walking. He was incredibly supportive of my decision and praised me for being a team player which made me feel somewhat better inside.

I arrived at the site with about 20 minutes of sunlight left in which to erect two tents. It had also begun to rain, and the wind was picking up. This was to be the first time I would be setting up my current tent properly (I had pitched it a few times at home to practice, but not in the dark).

With the rain getting heavier and heavier I said goodbye to my taxi driver and began to lug each of our bags across to a pitch which I thought maybe slightly sheltered by a tree. Turns out it wasn't!

I got the tents out and threw a poncho over the bags to prevent them getting soaked through. I was still wearing trainers on my feet which were getting drenched in the grass and my feet were gradually going numb. This was turning into a nightmare!

I took the decision to erect the tarpaulin (tarp)we had with us to create some form of shelter for our equipment whilst I put up the tents, this would also mean our tents weren't soaked in the morning. Under the light of my head torch I pinned one edge of the tarp into the floor and then used my walking poles to pitch out a 'lean to' type of structure. This was more difficult than it sounds and took me a good 20 minutes as the poles fell multiple times and the tarp would not stay taut. I was shivering and could no longer feel my feet. I managed to move all the bags under cover before starting to peg out my own tents 'inner'.

While the tarp was great for sheltering both me and the equipment from the rain it wasn't so great in terms of manoeuvrability. Due to lack of head room I had to crawl on my hands and knees to slide the poles into the tent and to peg out the outer layer. By the time I had finished I was drenched from head to toe, shivering and exhausted.

I threw my bag into the tent, collapsed into a heap, with steam radiating off me as I lay motionless trying to catch my breath. I curled up as tears of absolute exhaustion began to stream down my face. I couldn't feel my feet, my clothes were soaked through, I was shaking all over and felt drained of all energy.

After a while I pulled out my phone and rang Phil. I didn't say much, (I was too tired) but just hearing a friendly voice in the dark helped me calm down slightly. While on the phone a message came through from Dean telling me him and Rachael had stopped 2 miles short of the campsite. They had struggled for visibility and were drenched through so had found a B&B with a room available. They would meet me at the campsite at 08.00 the next morning. I was relived they were safe and replied saying that was fine, their bags were safe and dry, and I would see them in the morning.

I now focused on myself, on getting dry and warm, and on treating my feet, but only after first cleaning my teeth and getting ready for bed. Back out into the rain I went moving as quickly as I could to the toilet block. I knew a warm shower was what I needed but didn't have the energy to undress or dry myself, so I didn't bother. Once I had done my teeth etc. I hobbled back to my tent and removed my dripping wet clothes so I could switch into my thermals. Trying to do all this in a one-man tent with little space was difficult. The small amount of space not taken up by my sleeping mat and bag was taken up with my rucksack meaning there wasn't any real room for movement.

I finally managed to change and laid out my damp coat and waterproof trousers down the side of my sleeping mat, before stuffing all my other clothes into the bottom of my sleeping bag where my body heat would both dry them, and keep them warm (this was a trick I had learnt whilst climbing Mount Kilimanjaro).

Next, was to assess the situation with my feet. The blister that had been plaguing me all day was bigger than a few hours previous and was once again full of fluid; I popped it, applied iodine gel and covered it loosely with gauze. I also had a sore spot on the outside of my right foot caused by walking incorrectly to compensate for the blister. I followed the same process and covered up each blister one by one. I took a number of ibuprofens before putting my medical supplies away and then settled down to sleep.

I had a horrible night's sleep with the strong wind and rain. I woke multiple times worrying that the tarp had come down leaving Dean and Rachael's kit open to the elements. A few times I opened my tent door to check everything was secure and at one point without too much thought went out in my thermals to tighten up the ropes. It was a long, long night.

CHAPTER 18: 'MOO-VING' ALONG

I woke at around 07.30 next morning and didn't have long to get ready given that Dean and Rachael planned on being at the site for 08.00. I quickly set about packing away all the contents of my tent before tending to my blisters and covering them for the days walking. They didn't feel as tender to touch so hoped this would make the walking easier.

When I clambered out of my tent, I was relieved to find the tarp still standing, and the rucksacks still underneath it covered up by the poncho. Even better, I was no longer getting the sharp needle like pain each time I put my right food down; I could just feel a slight burning pain like that you get with a new blister. After the previous day's performance, I felt I could cope with that and began to feel confident for the day ahead.

We were now 2 days away from Bath and our first day off. Had anyone asked us though we would have said we were only 1 day away. To help keep us going we had decided that once a day had started that it no longer counted in our days to go. Today was Wednesday, we would arrive in Bath on Thursday, so we were now only 1 day away. Sound reasoning?

I felt much better than the previous day and given we had a short distance of 15 miles to do I felt hopeful I could survive another day. (Before undertaking the walk had anyone tried telling me 15 miles was a short distance to walk, I would have laughed, funny how your perspective can change so easily.)
Our day was no different to the previous days, the agenda being walk as far as possible in the morning, find somewhere to eat then repeat in the afternoon, suffer the 'hell miles' before then collapsing from exhaustion into our tents. That day we did have a moment of comic relief which broke the monotony. We climbed over a stile to find our path blocked by cows laid down all along the path and surrounding area. It was almost as though they knew we were coming and wanted to make their presence felt. All was not lost as we spotted a small path running parallel with a wall to the right-hand side of where we needed to be. We took this in the hope that it would join up with the original path only to be faced with yet another herd of cows relaxing. It was "Cow Armageddon" or 'Cow-mageddon'. We had no option but to carry on, moving slowly between each cow trying not to make any sudden movement, and at times we were close enough to feel the warmth from their nostrils. We didn't speak or make a sound as we slowly wound our way through the field in single file eventually reaching the other side to find our way blocked by a building! Dean found a gate we could climb over to get

out of the field safely, but which left us unsure whether we were on private property. We successfully made it out alive and without any prosecutions being served.

Most of the day was wet underfoot and I very quickly became aware my boots were no longer waterproof (despite re proofing them) as my feet were soaking wet. At our lunch stop I found a free newspaper and tucked it in my bag. That evening I would use it to stuff my shoes with to help them dry out.

Around 18.00 Dean announced we had about 15 minutes of walking time left; at this point we were in a large wood at the bottom of a hill heading towards our campsite. An hour later we were still walking. Dean was joking told he must no longer give us an approximation of time left to go.

We soon came to a halt when Dean announced the campsite should be visible. It wasn't. We were surrounded by tall trees and a stream. We continued to a clearing up ahead where we came across a couple of guys out walking. I enquired if they knew where the campsite was, they had a vague idea kindly led us up the hill saying the site was about a mile along the dirt track. Cue another 15 minutes of walking (not using Deans time frame here).

Finally, after what turned out to be more like a 20-mile day we arrived at our campsite, "Vallis Veg Farm Campsite", one which focused on being as eco-friendly as possible. They had compost toilets and minimal running-water. It was a different experience for us but one that seemed fitting for the 'challenge' we had undertaken. The staff were incredibly welcoming and had a campfire lit under a wooden shelter ready for our arrival; we felt quite rude being unable to spend much time around it due to utter exhaustion and our need for bed.

Once again it rained during the night but that didn't stop me getting a relatively good night's sleep. I awoke earlier than usual but given that the rain seemed to have stopped I decided to get everything packed away before hanging my tent over the wooden beams near the fire pit to dry. My tarp from the previous night was still damp so I pulled that out to dry. The shelter soon resembled a Chinese laundry.

Within a couple of hours later we were on our way, our motivation levels high as we would be reaching Bath that evening which meant we had a well-deserved day off to look forward to.

First things first we had to locate the path we had been on the day before which meant walking down a steep hill into the woods. As the sun hadn't yet risen it was pretty dark and visibility was poor. It didn't take long for Rachael to lose her footing, descend the hill on her bottom and end up covered in mud. Fortunately, she laughed it off and on we went.

If the previous day had become known as 'Cow-mageddon' then that day was going to become known as the day we invented "Field Bingo". During the day we climbed numerous stiles and walls in order to get into many different fields, grazed by a variety of animals. Whether it was sheep, cows and bulls, horses, alpacas or goats we walked with or by them all. As we moved from one field into another, we each had a go at guessing what animal would be in the next one. About 5 miles out of Bath we came across another field full of cows, unfazed at this point we made our way through feeling their warm breath once again as we snuck past to reach the other side where we came upon a lady, her gaze fixed on the cows, looking terrified. She asked if it had been okay walking through, so we gave her our best tips for navigating a field full of cows before saying our 'goodbyes' and continuing on our way. However, she then asked if one of us would accompany her across the field. Dean volunteered to guide the lady through the field whilst Rachael and I watched. We chuckled at the thought of what was happening, not at what we could see but the thought of what Dean would actually be able to do to help if all the cows decided to charge at once. Dean and the lady crossed the field without interruption. Mission 'protect the public from cows' now over we continued on towards Bath.

Once again, the last few miles of the day were horrible. We made our way through the outskirts of Bath with our muscles aching, our feet soaking wet and feeling completely exhausted. It was with some relief we managed to make it to the Youth Hostel which was to be our home for the next 2 nights. Given that there was no need to pitch a tent Rachael and I dumped our bags next to a bed each in our dormitory and straight away set about sorting out piles of washing. Once completed it was time to sort out our feet. Given that we had a day off from walking the next day I decided to take all plasters, 'Compeed' and tape off my feet giving then the chance to be fully cleaned and dried.

Rachael had developed what we later nick named 'the egg' on her ankle, a large white blister with what looked like a yellow centre. As she pressed on it white liquid seeped out from under the 'Compeed' plaster. I don't know what this says about us as people, but we were both excited at the prospect of her 'popping it'. We got out our supplies and laid out toilet roll on the floor to catch the 'gunk' that we anticipated exploding out of it once she removed the

'Compeed'. We were to be disappointed. Nothing 'exploded' out and once the dressing was off, we could see the blister had healed quite well. How boring!

I left Rachael to continue popping her blisters and set about sorting out my own feet. I began to remove the tape and 'Compeed' one bit at a time, first from the back of my ankles and then my toes. All was going well until it came to the inside of my right foot and the outside of my left ankle. As I slowly began to remove the 'Compeed' I could see the blister and skin underneath were beginning to come off as well. I jumped in the shower hoping the water would release the dressing from the blister and skin. It was hopeless and I ended up having to slowly cut away the dressing piece by piece with scissors. It was a long and painful process where at times it was hard to see the difference between compeed and skin.

Feet sorted, we headed to the laundry/drying room with our filthy gear. I hung my tent and tarp up as they were still damp and placed my filthy and drenched boots on a rack to dry. Next it was time for pizza at the bar and then an early night.

As we returned to our room, we got talking to a few of our roommates. One lady was from New Zealand and after asking what we were doing she amazingly donated £50 to our cause; such generosity was to be applauded. We immediately invited her to add a name to our white Quest for Brest T shirts. As part of our luggage each of us was carrying a white t-shirt, branded with our challenge logo that anyone (in exchange for a monetary donation) could write the name of a loved one on who had or was still battling cancer. The aim was to wear these t-shirts as we crossed the 'finish line' at the Piece Hall in Halifax.

CHAPTER 19: BATH TIME

We had a nice leisurely morning the next day before heading into Bath to visit one of the Roman Baths and stock up on supplies. We tried our best to get a massage each at the baths but unfortunately, they were fully booked up. I was gutted as having treatment on my right calf would have been beneficial as it still felt incredibly tight and sore from my blister fiasco a few days ago. It felt amazing at the baths to be immersed in warm water and to experience weightlessness. We did get some rather puzzled looks as we hobbled around with bruised feet and mangled toes.

After shopping for supplies and food we headed back to the youth hostel eager to get off our feet for the rest of the day. I had purchased some water proofer for my boots so having first washed them I then applied this before stuffing them again with newspaper to help them dry quicker.

We spent the remainder of our day re packing our bags and resting up in the bar area where we met a fellow walker on his way down to Lands' End from John O'Groats. He was a teacher who had taken a sabbatical to complete his epic journey. We talked at length about the similarities of our journeys, although his was double the length of ours (in miles) it seemed we were all experiencing the same things e.g. blisters, 'hell miles' and poor weather. His original plan had been to camp throughout his walk, but he had thrown away his tent after leaving Scotland due to the extra weight and was instead relying on B&B's. We were each in admiration of the others journey, us of him because he was walking for longer and on his own, him of us in that we were carrying all our equipment and had started in a different country.

So we didn't wake the others in our room with our early departure Rachael and I prepared our bags as much as we could that evening and eventually turned in at 22.30 which was rather late for us (we had been in bed most nights before 20.00). We awoke naturally at around 06.00 and snuck out of the dormitory. We sat in the corridor to make our final preparations and applied all our tape, mole skin and 'Compeed' to our feet before heading down for breakfast. We were the only people in the eating area and the staff were asking us what we were doing, as was now to be expected they were shocked, told us we were mad but wished us well on our journey.

There were a couple of things making the idea of walking again bearable to me that day and helped to motivate me a) Phil and my mother and father in law (Steve and Jackie) would be arriving that same day to walk with us the next day and b) we had another day of less than 20 miles to do. However, first things first! We had to walk through Bath itself and up the giant hill at the other side of the city. This seemed to take an age as we walked through the streets, past several local shops and housing estates. On reflection Bath was a beautiful place and I wish we could have spent more time there.

After about 2 hours we had successfully made it out of Bath, and we were back into the sticks and onto the Cotswold Way. I had heard many good things about this trail and was looking forward to the views and hopefully a clear path throughout. We weren't to be disappointed as we walked through some beautiful villages and rolling fields.

At one point as we were walking along a ridge line, we spotted a group of people in the field below, the loud noises we could hear helped us identify them as a group of clay pigeon shooters who quickly put up their guns as we passed. We could sense their eyes watching us in frustration as we scurried past them as fast as we could however, we had to come to a stop as there was a fork in the path. Both options were signposted the Cotswold Way. It took us a few minutes to decide that the path going downwards was the one we needed. Still feeling the eyes burning into the back of our heads we picked up our pace and headed downwards to the sound of shooting guns.

Before long we came across another couple of walkers heading in the opposite direction, with large rucksacks on their back. It was clear they had been walking for a while, so we stopped for a quick chat. He was from South Africa and she was from England; they had always wanted to walk the Cotswold Way and were finally managing to doing so. They were overjoyed when we told them they were only a few hours away from Bath, their finishing point. They had completed the whole trail in 13 days and were astounded to hear we were doing it in 4 days. We wished them well and went on our way only to realise a few minutes later that the clay pigeon shooters guns had suddenly stopped so the couple must have come across them like we had done.

We continued walking and during the next mile came across several groups of walkers, each heading into Bath. We suddenly realised the impact these walkers were going to have upon the clay pigeon shooters and how irate they must be feeing at being interrupted. In all fairness taking part in a shoot on the edge of the Cotswold Way, one of the most famous and popular trails in England did seem rather silly.

Our day was going brilliantly, and we were marking off the mileage. By 14.00 we only had 7 miles left to go so I contacted Steve and Jackie to let them know how we were getting on. I asked what time they expected to arrive at the camp site to which they replied they were 80 miles away in their campervan and stuck in traffic. Phil contacted me to say he was just setting off and was 160 miles away. At this point it seemed as though we had been dropped into a Top Gear challenge as to who was going to arrive at the end point first, us on foot with the least mileage to cover, Phil in the powerful Audi with the most mileage to cover or Steve and Jackie in the slightly slower (but still faster than walking) campervan. The race was on! The gauntlet had been thrown!

Disappointingly but not unsurprisingly we didn't win the race, although had we not stopped off at a pub for a quick drink it turned out we probably would have. Steve and Jackie had already arrived at Cotswold Meadow Glamping when we arrived. I had made prior contact with the owner asking if we would be able to pitch our tents for the night given that it was only for glamping tents. She had replied saying she would put us up in one of her bell tents free of charge because we were doing the walk for charity.

It was great to see Steve and Jackie and we walked to our tent, we filled them in on our journey so far. Phil was still some way off, so we had a quick nap while we waited for him to arrive. We went through the normal routine of treating our feet and sorting out our equipment. My feet appeared to be fine overall, there had been some slight rubbing on the little toe of my right foot, but no blister had formed yet. I planned to cover it for the next day of walking.

A few hours later Phil arrived, and we all made our way into the nearest town to find some good food before heading to bed.

CHAPTER 20: A FRIENDLY VISIT

As I lay in bed the next morning all I could hear was rain thrashing down on the roof. Great! We had 23 miles to walk and in terms of ascent it was going to the toughest yet. If the rain continued at this volume, we would be soaked within minutes of setting off.

Once we were all up we discussed what we should do and having consulted the weather forecast decided to put back our start time for the day until 10.00 in the hope that the worst of the rain would have passed over, however this would leave us short on time to complete our mileage for the day. To enable us to walk at a faster pace we decided to leave all our bags with Jackie in the camper van. That evening we were staying in an apartment so a late arrival in the dark wouldn't be as much of a problem given that there would be no tents to put up.

I had asked Phil to bring along my walking shoes and I decided to give these another go. Given the weather I still had doubts as to whether or not my walking boots were currently watertight (despite having re-proofed them in Bath) and blisters hadn't really been a big issue for me in France with them on, so it was certainly worth a try.

We finally set off around 10.30. It was great to have Phil, Steve and their dog Rum walking with us for the day as it brought a different dynamic to the group and new conversation. Despite our plan for a faster walking pace (minus our bags) this didn't come to fruition. The hills, fields and woods we had to walk through meant our pace remained at our 'normal rate' of around 2.5 miles per hour.

We met Jackie with the campervan at lunch time. Despite wanting to put our feet up for hours we knew time was precious so instead quickly ate our food. Just before we set off again, I had a quick look at my toe, a blister was now starting to come through, so I covered it with 'Compeed'. At this point it was annoying rather than painful.

Once again, we were on our way. As the day wore on the pressure to keep up a fast pace began to cause tension within the group and any request to take a short break was likely to cause friction. I just tried to keep my head down, persevere with the walking and ignore the throbbing pain I could feel in my toe.

We were walking through a local town when a car started tooting its horn at us, I looked up, a little confused as to why we were being beeped at. It was when the car pulled up onto the nearest pavement that I realised it was 2 of my friends from back home in West Yorkshire; Laura and Rebecca, who were heading down south for a holiday. They had consulted our Spot tracker on our website and realised that our route would go somewhere near theirs so had taken a slight detour to try to come and find us. It was great to see them and lovely to hear that they had driven out of their way to find us. They brought some much-needed relief to the day. We stopped and chatted to them for around 10 minutes during which I was able to redress the blister on my toe as I could feel the 'Compeed' slipping off. I sat on the pavement, removed my socks to see that the blister had now risen up into a nice big lump on my toe. I popped this and then covered it with a smaller 'Compeed' that wrapped nicely around my toe. All too soon we had to say our reluctant 'goodbyes' to Laura and Rebecca and get back on our way.

It was late afternoon; the light was starting to fade, and we still had a long way to go. You could have cut the tension with a knife as we all walked on in silence. I soon accepted we would be walking till dark and that there was nothing we could really do about it. Trying to maintain a pace quicker than the one we were keeping was nigh on impossible and would only put more strain on our already sore bodies.

We had our final rest stop for the day at around 19.00 and we still had 6 miles to walk. It was at this point that Steve pulled out his second large family sized bar of Cadburys Milk Chocolate. We devoured it within minutes! The night was now closing in and soon we were walking in the dark, head torches on we walked in single file down the side of a road. It wasn't a fun walk, as traffic speeded on by. I suggested we try and get off the road and try to find an alternative route. As it happened there was woodland path which we decided to take. It would be darker but safer.

By 20.00 we were onto moorland and we could see the faint lights of Stroud in the distance. On and on we went hardly able to make each other out in the dark. As ever the 'hell miles' set in. I began to feel a stabbing pain in my Achilles again, pain I hadn't felt since leaving France. I concluded it must be the shoes I was wearing that were causing the problems since once I had switched to my walking boots in Poole, I hadn't been troubled by it.

Our accommodation for the night was of course at the far side of Stroud, so we had to find our way through the town before finally reaching the apartment. None of us had any energy left to actually go out for a meal so Phil and Steve went to collect some Domino's pizza which we couldn't wait to devour and on arrival ate very quickly before getting ready for bed.

Due to the problems I was having with my feet and Achilles I wasn't sure what footwear I should now use. My walking shoes had served me well that day as regards blisters but the pain they seemed to be causing to my Achilles was worrying me however, on the other hand my walking boots didn't seem to be waterproof, were not as comfortable as my walking shoes but they didn't cause pain in my legs. There was no obvious choice so I decided I would simply carry both with me. I didn't really want to carry the extra weight but sending one pair home with Phil seemed a risk too big to take in the circumstances. What if I made the wrong choice? Once Phil left my mistake couldn't be rectified.

Phil helped me repack my bag with the extra shoes in before he left. Again saying 'goodbye' to Phil, Jackie and Steve was incredibly hard and left me feeling lost and dejected. It was already late, so I decided to just head for bed.

The next morning as tried to get my feet into my walking shoes it became obvious that my feet and heels had swollen up again. I tied my shoes up and my feet felt as though they were in a vice. I had to take them off as there was no way I could walk in them. I switched back into my boots, putting my walking shoes at the top of my bag. It seemed I had made a good decision last night to carry both my walking boots and walking shoes with me!

Once on route we fell into our normal routine and despite a lot of uphill and muddy tracks we had a decent day. We stopped at a pub for lunch where we checked the weather forecast for that night and the next day. Our initial plan had been to reach a campsite on the outskirts of Cheltenham where we would stay the night and then have the next day off from walking, however thunderstorms and torrential downpours were forecast for the next 48 hours and this made us re-think our plans. We pulled out our Ordnance Survey maps and then started looking on booking.com for any cheap hotels in Cheltenham. Luckily for us the local YMCA Youth Hostel had rooms available and staying there would knock a few miles off our day. A result! Feeling motivated to continue we left the pub and completed our last 2 miles into Cheltenham. It had been a good day.

The Youth Hostel was pretty run down and when we saw the receptionist lock up the front door before showing us to our rooms, we wondered how safe a place it was. Having said that we didn't really intend on leaving the room much, so we figured we would probably be fine.

Feeling the need to rest up as much as possible we ordered a takeaway from 'Just Eat'. When the drive arrived an hour later, I went out to meet him. As he passed me the food, he enquired whether I worked at the hostel and when I replied that I didn't he muttered something under his breath which sounded like a suggestion that I should grab my friends and get out of there as quickly as possible. I was so taken aback by what I thought he had said that before I could ask him to repeat himself, he had gone. Once back in the room I told Rachael and Dean what had happened and before we went to bed Rachael took the time to jam all our rucksacks in front of the door to prevent anyone forcing their way in. To be fair our 3 bags probably weighed nearly 40 kg between them so trying to force the door open would have been made a little more difficult.

It's safe to say we made it through the night unharmed and of course we all joked how this was clearly only due to Rachael's rucksack blockade.

We spent our day off doing little other than going into town to get the now essential newspaper for wet boots, more 'Compeed' and food. I was still having some discomfort from my little toe whilst walking but any 'Compeed' or tape I put on kept falling off with sweat and movement. I managed to find a box of corn plasters that you put over your toes which I bought thinking one could go over the top of my dressings to help keep them on. Just another thing to add to the foot treatment routine.

Having tried but having to abandon wearing my walking shoes the previous day I now decided to post them home to Phil having first found an outdoor shop where I managed to buy some waterproof socks to wear with my boots. All purchases made we spent the rest of the day laid in bed at the Youth Hostel, staying off our feet as much as possible.

During the night I was woken up by a throbbing feeling in my little toe; at this point little did I know this was a warning for what was soon to come.

CHAPTER 21: BREAK POINT

Surprisingly, I awoke the next morning feeling refreshed and raring to go. Unfortunately, our day didn't get off to the best start, as for the first time on the whole trip we went the wrong way, over a mile in the wrong direction to be exact. Frustrated about the time and energy wasted we turned back and picked up a new route.

Most of our day was spent walking through large fields that seemed to get muddier and muddier as we went. Our feet became ladened down by what felt like half the field sticking to the bottom of our shoes. We promptly stated a poll on social media as to who had managed to get the most mud on their feet. As the day went on, I was becoming more and more aware of the pain in my little toe, a throbbing sensation that was uncomfortable to walk on.

Our end point for the day was a camp site called Wold End Farm in the small town of Chipping Camden. On arrival we saw exactly why people talk of how beautiful a place Chipping Camden is. The streets were full of quirky independent shops and the whole town had a picture-perfect feel to it. It's an absolute haven for walkers as it comes right at the end of the Cotswold trail.

Wold End Farm was a caravan only sight during the season but prior to departure I had made contact with the owners who had agreed to us pitching our tents on a small patch of grass in addition to us using the toilet in their outhouse. We were incredibly thankful to them as this had meant we could stay on route instead of deviating miles off route just to find somewhere to stay.

It was an incredibly cold evening and I couldn't stop shivering as I pitched my tent and got ready for bed, I was layered up to the max with thermals a fleece and my jacket on. I just wanted to curl up in my sleeping bag but knew I needed to look at my feet. I looked at them only to discover a new blister on the inside of my right foot at the bottom of my big toe. I could only assume I had been walking on the inside of my foot rather than my full foot to avoid causing more damage to my little toe. Great, I now had another blister to add to my collection I treat them all as quickly as possible before wrapping myself up in my sleeping bag and shivering myself to sleep. I woke up during the night needing to put a few extra layers on. I knew if any part of my body wasn't fully covered by my sleeping bag, I would immediately start shivering, so I cocooned myself in. Despite my best efforts I had a pretty rough night's sleep.

It was still extremely cold the next morning so instead of getting dressed in my tent I grabbed all my clothes and headed for the toilet which was marginally warmer. Once dressed I returned to dismantle my tent which was still wet with dew. I hung it across some nearby logs, wiped it down to try and dry it off a bit, (after all a wet tent is a heavier tent and I didn't want to have to carry any extra weight) before eating my breakfast.

We set off for the day and while I was very conscious of the throbbing pain in my little toe and on the inside of my foot, once we were up and walking the pain was bearable. The problem was whenever we stopped the pain of getting going again was a lot to handle. My feet plagued me all day, but I tried my best to just keep going.

After a quick lunch break, we came across a new obstacle, a recently dug up field. Our route showed there would be a clear path through the field, but this was no longer the case. Whoever owned the field had now made it look more like something you see on pictures of the Somme during World War 1.

With no option but to cross it Rachael took a couple of tentative steps and found the mud was relatively firm, so we all started to make our way across. It was exceptionally difficult for me, on every step I could feel either the blisters on the outside or the inside of my foot hitting against my shoe, causing a sharp shooting pain. The faster I went the more pain it caused. In the end I must have looked like someone trying to run across hot coals as I kept my feet on the floor as little as possible.

That obstacle navigated it was time for the next one, a stream that was several feet wide and deep. Under normal circumstances I don't think any of us would have battered an eyelid at having to leap across it but with heavy rucksacks on our backs and mud-covered steep banking's we stopped to work out our options. Ultimately there was no alternative than to make the leap and hope for the best. I lined myself up and took a small run before pushing off the banking with one foot and throwing myself onto the ground at the other side. I had a vision of me landing but then tipping over backwards due to the weight of my rucksack, so I figured a close up with the floor was preferable to ending up in the water. We all made it over safely but in a bizarre way there was almost a sense of disappointment that at least one of us hadn't slipped in and provided an opportunity for a good laugh at someone's expense, but hey that's friends for you!

Obstacles now completed for the day it was a steady walk (albeit in the rain) to our next campsite at Church Hall farm. As we arrived at the site the owner was just walking around, we introduced ourselves and he then informed us one of their overnight huts was free if we wanted to upgrade to that. He very kindly offered us a big discount on his charges when he realised the challenge we were undertaking was for charity. We took him up on the offer straight away, after all a night in a hut was going to be much better than another night spent in a tent in the rain. So, we piled into a small room with two bunkbeds, had showers, ate some food and treated our feet before going to bed.

Sadly, that night I had the worst sleep of the whole trip lying awake for hours before finally drifting off. My feet were throbbing intensely, and I couldn't get comfortable. Both feet felt as though they had a heartbeat of their own. I kept trying to put them in different positions hoping to alleviate some of the pain, but it was no good. I scrambled down from my bunk and dug out some Ibuprofen which must have helped as I eventually nodded off hours later.

When I woke up the next morning, I could still feel my feet throbbing so I knocked back a few more Ibuprofen tablets as soon as I could. I knew there and then that day was going to be a real struggle.

Before I put my boots on, I checked my feet over during which I noticed that my little toe was looking very purple, the blister on the inside of my foot was very raw and in general they looked incredibly swollen. I cleaned and covered them the best I could. Putting my boots on was becoming more and more painful. If any of the blisters encountered the rim of the boots as I slid my feet into them, I knew about it and it took me some time to get my feet in to a somewhat comfortable position.

Once my feet were in my boots I stood up and threw my bag over my shoulders. I could stand with minimal pain so maybe all hope wasn't lost, and I would be able to walk. As we set off it soon became clear that this wasn't going to be the case as each step I took I was getting sharp stabbing pains on both sides of my feet. We hadn't even made it to the top of the driveway before I had to sit down and redress my feet. Once done, I felt marginally better and we continued on, but the pain soon came flooding back.

I was very aware of the need to keep a good pace and I didn't want to let the team down, so I adapted my walking style to using only the heel of my right foot. While this was still painful it meant I could go a bit faster as I limped along bringing up the rear.

At about 5 miles into the day and while in the middle of a field I reached breaking point. The pain was now unbearable, and I just needed to get off my feet. I looked down at my boots and was shocked to see that they were actually coming apart at the seams near my little and big toes. I was quite literally walking myself out of my boots due to the swelling in my feet. I had to keep moving, having an emotional breakdown in the middle of a field was not going to help anyone, so we changed track and slowly made our way towards the nearest town called Wootton Wawen. On the outskirts we came across a sign for the train station and came to a stop. I knew there and then that I should call it a day, that I should just accept I couldn't continue. Seeing the state of my boots Rachael and Dean suggested I stopped for the day, went to the hotel and treated my feet before they got any worse. We all knew I didn't want to, but it was the logical thing to do so I agreed to it. We made our way towards the train station and agreed our plan of action. Rachael wanted to stay with me to ensure I got to the hotel safely, I assured her I would be fine and that she should keep walking. I didn't want her to have to stop or miss miles because of me and navigating trains in an unknown place didn't bother me at all.

We agreed to rendezvous at the Premier Inn that evening before I gave Dean the spot tracker and bid them both on their way. Next job I had to figure out exactly where I was and where I needed to be. It didn't take me long. I simply had to catch a train from this station into Birmingham and then from there another train out to Berkswell which was 1.5 miles away from the Premier Inn. The next train wasn't for half an hour, but it didn't matter I wasn't in a major rush and at least it meant I could just sit down for a while and wait. I spent some time ringing Phil and my parents to update them on what was happening. I sat in the station with tears rolling down my face feeling like a complete failure.

Once the train arrived it took around 40 minutes to get into Birmingham itself. I sat there covered in mud with walking poles and a huge rucksack looking somewhat dishevelled and read the Metro newspaper to pass the time. My spirits were lifted when I spotted a full page spread dedicated to Celine Dion's upcoming world tour, with me and Phil being fans I googled tickets thinking it would be a nice way to celebrate finishing the walk. My spirits hit rock bottom again when I saw they were £150 each. Never mind.

Next I had to walk through Birmingham itself to get to the next station. Brilliant more walking! Thankfully, it wasn't too great a distance and about an hour later I was stumbling off the second train at Berkswell station. I felt like a fraud ordering an uber taxi to take me 1.5 miles up the road to the hotel, but I just wasn't capable of walking any further.

I was a bit early for 'check in' but thankfully the receptionist took pity on me, gave me my key and arranged for a bucket of ice to be brought up to my room. Once inside, I ran a cold bath and threw the ice in before placing my feet into it. I did this several times throughout the rest of the day as room service were kind enough to keep bringing me buckets.

I spent some time thinking and planning for the remainder of the walk, we had one more day of walking before a planned day off near Drayton Manor. Plan A: My feet would make a miraculous recovery; I would spring out of bed the next morning and be able to continue on. Plan B: I would see if the hotel had a room available for a 2nd night, I would then have two full days off my feet which would give them a better chance of healing before having to start walking again from Drayton Manor. Plan C: I called it a day and gave up completely. I didn't like and wasn't willing to consider plan C; Plan A seemed less realistic given the amount of pain I was in at the time; but Plan B seemed possible. I went down to ask the receptionist if they had any rooms available for the next night, unfortunately they didn't however, the receptionist advised me to download the Premier Inn app and keep checking on there for room cancellations. Apparently, there was a major equestrian event going on at the NEC in Birmingham and all rooms in the area were booked up but if I was lucky someone may cancel.

I kept checking for cancellations throughout the day, but nothing came up. I spent much of the day laid down on the bed to keep my weight and pressure off my feet as much as possible. I showered before laying my tent and any wet gear out across the floor and then turned the heating up to maximum to help dry my equipment out.

It was a long, boring day and minutes passed like hours. After a considerably long time Dean and Rachael finally arrived at the Premier Inn. We met in the restaurant for food where I told them about my 3 plans of action. There were still no vacancies at our current hotel, so at this point I would have to go for plan A. I agreed to contact them in the morning to confirm whether I would be walking with them or not.

I completed one last ice bath treatment for my feet, did one last check on the app for vacancies (still no rooms available) and headed to bed.

The next morning, I woke up extremely early, around 04.00 so immediately looked at my phone to check the app for room vacancies. To my delight a room had become available for that night which I quickly booked, with the option of cancellation should my feet feel alright to walk on later on and then and went back to bed.

It was about 06.30 when I eventually swung my legs out of bed. The moment of truth had dawned (excuse the pun); would I be able to walk? I put my feet on the floor and the pain just came flooding back. I put my feet into my shoes and attempted to walk around the room, but the pain was still there. It was impossible, I couldn't put one foot in front of the other without wincing! I wasn't going anywhere that day! I rang Dean to tell him I was unable to walk, and I was now going with plan B. He and Racheal would do the miles for the day and heads towards Drayton Manor campsite where I would meet them the next morning. Phil had previously arranged to join us on our day off and would be arriving that evening so he would drive me to meet them.

I hobbled down to breakfast before returning to my room to ice my feet once again. It was at this point that I took a good look at them. My little toe was turning increasingly purple/black by the second! On closer inspection I could see yellow pus seeping out from the blister below it. It looked horrendous and hurt to touch. The blister on the inside of my foot was purple but thankfully not seeping. I checked 'Google' to see if I could find a pharmacy close by that I could visit and ask for advice. There was one a mile down the road, so I dressed and slowly made my way down to it. I couldn't bring myself to get a taxi for a distance of a mile.

Once at the Pharmacy I was told to wait outside the consultation room where the pharmacist would look at my feet. I sat down and removed my trainers and socks. The pharmacist took one look at my toes and told me that my blisters were infected. Not what I needed or wanted to hear! He advised me to buy some TCP and stay off my feet until they healed. I explained that may be a slight problem as I was currently in the middle of a 500-mile walk, but that I did have that day and the next off. He didn't look convinced as he replied that would be better than nothing. He told me I should stay on top of keeping the blisters clean and rest as much as possible.

I returned to the hotel where I spent the rest of my day switching between putting my feet into bowls of ice or TCP. Slowly the swelling on my feet began to go down. My decision not to walk had certainly been justified. Who knows what would have happened had I continued to push myself past my natural limit? I would be lying if I didn't say I thought I may have ended up losing my toe had I kept on going.

Things were now looking up, and I started to feel all hope wasn't lost. I just had one major problem to solve, footwear. With my boots split open at the seams they were no longer useable. I had my trusty pair of Nike trainers which I had used in France, but they weren't waterproof, and with my feet in such a state I couldn't actually bear to wear them as they were now so tight and uncomfortable. The only other footwear I had in my bag was flip flops, not exactly hiking/walking footwear.

I decided to consult both Phil and my parents about my problem. As Phil was arriving that evening he had agreed to bring my walking shoes, and his own walking boots for me to try. My Mum suggested she drove down the next day with a selection of walking shoe/boots from home. It seemed ridiculous that she was only a 2-hour drive away from where I was, but that was 6/7 days of walking for us. I readily accepted both offers of help in the hope that one of the pairs of shoes/boots would fit and be comfortable on my very deformed feet. I would also go to the shops to try to find a better and more comfortable pair of trainers that I could use as last resort.

My plan was put into action the next day when Phil and I went to the nearest retail area. I tried on multiple pairs of trainers but initially struggled to find anything comfortable. Eventually I came across a pair that were a size bigger than I would normally wear but which felt comfortable and didn't put pressure on my toes. A bonus was they had good thick soles and if push came to shove would be comfortable for walking in over the next week.

My Mum arrived as planned, along with my brother and 'Auntie'. We had a meal together before looking at the selection of walking boots/shoes they had brought with them. I first tried on the shoes I had used in France, but they were far too tight and uncomfortable; multiple other pairs were too big. I finally settled on a pair of my Mums that felt comfortable to wear and didn't cause any pain as I moved, even with my blisters as they were. I knew it was going to be a big risk to walk in these given I had never worn them before, but I didn't really have any other option. So, I bought several new rolls of tape and 'Compeed' to enable me to cover up any susceptible areas before I even started walking the next day.

That evening Phil and I made our way to Drayton Manor campsite where we put up my own, and Dean and Rachael's tent. They had left their rucksacks with me in the hotel the previous day to make their walk easier and had opted to stay overnight in a B & B about 6 miles away from Drayton Manor. They were now on their way to this evening's campsite, but it was getting dark and starting to rain so finding their tent already up meant they could at least get dry and warm on their arrival.

I bid Phil a difficult farewell, set to cleaning my feet with TCP and went to bed.

CHAPTER 22: ON THE ROAD AGAIN

Again, I woke incredibly early the next morning but instead of going back to sleep I dragged my gear out of my tent, collapsed it and headed for the toilet block. I thought I may as well use this time to make sure I cleaned my feet and prepped them as best I could for the day ahead and the shower block provided more room to do this.

I reapplied new 'Compeed' plasters to the heels and soles of both feet, cleaned and taped up my toes with gauze and KT Tape, and then rubbed Vaseline between my toes. I taped over the plasters to help keep them all in place. When we had met with Jackie and Steve, Jackie had given us all some silicone gel socks to go on our heels and balls of our feet to help stop blisters. They had worked well on my heels over the past week, so I put these on top of the KT tape. My feet were so well covered up and protected it almost felt like I could have set off there and then without any shoes on. I felt confident I had done everything I could to prep my feet ready for another week of walking. When I put the new boots on my feet felt snug and comfortable for the first time in weeks!

Rachael and Dean were soon awake, and we set off walking at around 07.30. It felt so good to be back with them and while I still felt annoyed at having missed some walking miles, I knew my decision had been sensible and was the reason I was able to walk that day.

Spurred on by all being back together we kept a fantastic pace all day, we had a quick stop for lunch in the city of Lichfield, where I cleaned and redressed the blister on my little toe. Just before leaving the area we spotted a Halifax Building Society, cue the jokes about finishing there as we had made it to Halifax.

Our morale was high and as we continued to walk through the city we soon came across and incredible and very rustic cathedral. We stood outside in amazement at the incredible architecture and spoke of how amazing it was that something like that could be built so many years ago without the use of the machinery we have now. It wasn't long before there was a steady stream of people arriving and heading inside, it didn't seem like anyone had tickets, so we followed the crowd in the general direction of the cathedral's entrance. It turned out we had walked in on a primary school harvest festival.

There we were stood at the back of this beautiful building in waterproof gear, splattered in mud with huge rucksacks on our backs listening to a large group of children sing 'Autumn Leaves' at the top of their voices. It wasn't long before a member of staff spotted us (after all we did stand out) and came to ask if we needed help, after a quick conversation with him we left armed with a variety of leaflets and information on topics such the cathedral's history and pilgrimages.

As we left the city of Lichfield behind us, we merrily discussed our harvest festival memories and spent the next hour singing old primary school songs, it certainly helped to pass the time.

We kept good pace and were closing in on our next campsite by about 15.00. It was at this point that I began to feel some rubbing on the back of my heels and the top of my big toes. I pulled over to check out my feet and applied some tape around my toes which were beginning to look quite red and sore. I already had 'Compeed' plasters, tape, silicon pads and socks on my heels so there wasn't much more protection I could apply so I simply had to continue on. I was getting to the point where walking and being in pain came hand in hand; it was the new 'normal' and I just had to deal with it.

Once at the campsite we managed to upgrade ourselves again, this time to a safari tent. As it hadn't been thoroughly prepared for guests, we got it at a heavily discounted price, but we weren't fussed, after all we looked in a far worse state than any tent. I was so relieved to be off my feet again and began to assess the damage. It was worse than I'd thought. I had two brand new large blisters on each heel, one blister on the top of each of my big toes and the blister on the inside of my right foot that had begun to heal was once again a white liquid filled lump. I wanted to scream and shout, this was beyond ridiculous, all I wanted was one day of pain free walking, was that too much to ask for? How I had managed to get blisters on my heels despite such heavy dressing I had no idea.

I proceeded to remove the tape I had applied to my toes earlier in the day as it had moved considerably. This was easier said than done, as I pulled the tape off my skin began to come with it. I was in agony! As was now the norm I dipped my safety pin in hand sanitizer and proceeded to pop each individual blister, before applying iodine cream on top of it and covering them with gauze.

Feet somewhat sorted, we decided to call an uber taxi to take us into the nearby town where we had noticed a Tesco superstore. Our safari tent had a microwave, so we'd decided to treat ourselves to a warm tea. Once we arrived at Tesco, we asked the driver to wait so he could take us back to the site. He agreed on the basis that we took no more than 2.5 minutes, then he wouldn't have to charge us. Cue a hobbling charge around the shop and amazingly we made it out of the shop with seconds to spare.

Back at the site we crowded round the small table to eat before bidding each other good night. It was another cold evening, so I cocooned myself in my sleeping bag praying for a miracle recovery for my feet.

In the morning there had been no miracle. I swung my feet out of bed and felt the now all too familiar stinging and stabbing pain in my feet. I was so disheartened because we had 23 miles to walk which was going to be agony. I took the time to re drain and clean all my blisters before applying 'Compeed' onto each one. My feet (now more 'Compeed' than skin) stung as I tied my boots in place. I walked out of the tent in silence, wondering how on earth I was going to get through the day. Every step I took I just wanted to burst into tears. I had suffered with so many blisters on the trip but so far, the pain had been contained to one foot or one particular area of my feet, this time it was everywhere and there was no escaping it.

I had no idea how I was going to manage the day, but I told myself to just try and get to the first town and take it from there. I downed 4 paracetamol and off we went. For the first mile or so every step was tentative as I tried to ease myself into the pain. It reminded me of when a bath is far too hot for you to get in, so you lower yourself in one bit at a time allowing yourself to acclimatise to it. I slowly increased the amount of pressure put onto each foot as I got used to the pain. We made it the first town and carried on, I just kept telling myself not to stop and just keep moving.

After 7 miles of agony and holding back tears I asked to stop. I was so tired and just needed to be pain free if only for a few minutes. As soon as I spoke up, we all stopped and immediately sat down. It became apparent we all felt the same, each of us had our own individual ailments and each of us needed to stop. We only stopped for 10 minutes but it was heaven! I took off my boots and socks to find that under the 'Compeed' the blisters on top of my toes were now huge and white with yellow liquid coming out from beneath which had formed a hard crust, I took the time to wipe them down as much as I could, it was delightful. All I wanted to do was to sit there all day and not move another muscle. Had we not been in a field and near a road I would have been very tempted to have stopped for good. Instead I gritted my teeth, got up onto my feet and carried on.

We carried on and on through fields of cows, at one point being followed/chased by a herd that had broken through their protective fencing. On our travels we had successfully negotiated walking through fields of various type of animal, crossed many streams/rivers and stood in ridiculous amounts of mud but what we passed through next took our experiences to a whole new level.

After crossing yet another field we arrived at a large silver gate to see before us what can only be described as a pig's bath. Our path was completely saturated with cow manure and there was no way around it. Dean reluctantly climbed over the fence first and set a path for us to follow, slowly meandering his way through the sea of 'poo'. Rachael went ahead of me using her walking stick to test the depth of the poo in front of her as she went. The stench was horrific, and it took great levels of concentration just to put one foot in front of the other. Suddenly Rachael disappeared in front of me as one of her feet was swallowed up in a mound of cow manure. As horrible as it was none of us could stop laughing as we pulled her out. Her foot was covered with it and as she was only wearing walking shoes the poo had managed to seep over the lip and into her socks. We christened this event 'Poo gate" which will remain in our memories forever.

During the next hour as we continued to make our way through the field of 'poo' we were kept amused by what had happened to Rachael. 'Poo gate' had slowed us down tremendously but it had provided some entertainment and helped me to forget the ever-throbbing pain in my feet if only for a moment.

We walked 15 miles before stopping for a late lunch and to stock up on newspapers to help dry out Rachael's shoes. After this it took me a while to get going again and ease myself into the pain of walking. Our route was now mostly uphill on tracks as we left the muddy fields behind and because of this I decided to switch into my trainers to give my feet a bit of a rest from the constant battering that the boots were giving them. My trainers felt much more comfortable and even though I could still feel the pain it was more bearable. For the first time that day I felt like I could make it to the end.

We were now only 3 miles away from our B&B for the night. I had almost done it. There was no way at the start of the day that I thought I would make it to the end. I thought the blisters would have beaten me, and defeated, I would have had to give up. Despite everything, I was going to make it!!!!

Trainers on we moved off and followed the winding road up towards the town of Alton. As we turned the first corner, I let out a sigh! There about halfway up the road was a chuffing ford. I had just changed out of my waterproof boots into my non waterproof trainers and now we had to cross a ford. I couldn't believe our luck! Dean walked straight through. Rachael followed taking the opportunity to wash off the cow pat and meanwhile I stood there laughing. It was the first time for weeks that I had found some shoes that were comfortable on my feet and we now had to cross a ford. There was no way I could avoid it or avoid getting my shoes wet.

A car soon pulled up and slowed down next to me so much so that I thought the driver was going to offer me a lift across the water, instead he took one look at me and darted on through the water. Charming.

Dean jokingly suggested going through bare foot, so guess what, that's exactly what I did. I stripped off my socks and shoes and began to make my way through the water. It was probably about a foot deep and a was slippery underfoot but goodness it felt good on my feet! Once on the other side I sat down to dry my feet off. I knew what I had just done hadn't necessarily been good for my infected blisters, but boy, had it felt good on my swollen and tender feet.

On arrival in Alton we quickly found our B&B and headed straight to our room. The owner of the B&B looked at us with some confusion when we simply collapsed onto the floor in a heap and didn't say much to her or each other. I lay still whilst smiling to myself. I had made it! I felt like I had overcome so much to get here. Privately, I was so proud of myself. Having suffered some of the worst physical pain in my life I had actually done it!

CHAPTER 23: RECALCULATIONS

There were now only 4 days of walking remaining, the end was now near. Our next stop was to be Leek where we had scheduled in a day of rest before undertaking 3 days walking which covered substantial mileage and included numerous steep ascents.

Our finals 4 days consisted of a 16.6 mile walk to Leek followed by a rest day; a 25.5 mile day which included 4246 metres of accent to Disley; a penultimate day that would cover 23.10 miles with 4339 metres of accent to Marsden before our final day of 12 miles into Halifax.

Given that our biggest day so far had been 24 miles in France with little to no ascent we knew the remaining days would be a challenge. When I had planned the route, I had known these days were ambitious hence us having a day off in Leek which would allow us to make slight changes to the route if necessary.

I had been doing some calculations in my head as to how best to utilise our day off to minimise some of the mileage we had still to cover. I suggested to Dean and Rachael that we discuss our plans for the next few days that evening.

My suggestion was once we had arrived in Leek (16.6 miles way) the next day that we set up our tents, have some food before then walking a further 5 miles thus reducing our mileage for the following day. We would then return to our campsite to sleep. On our day off we could then walk approximately 10-11 miles before returning to Leek again and resting up for the remainder of the day. The day following our planned "day off", originally planned as a 25.5 mile day, would be then reduced to a mere 15 miles so we could round this up to 20/21 by walking a bit further and take a taxi to our already booked hotel in Disley. I don't know if Dean and Rachael understood immediately (or if you the reader does) but we all agreed that it sounded both logical and sensible. So, our revised plan was set. The remainder of our journey looking as follows:

Day	Original Plan	Revised Plan (with approximate mileage)
26	Alton to Leek: 16.60 miles	Alton to Leek: 16.60 miles + 5 miles extra done in the evening
27	Day Off	Wherever we stopped walking the previous day to Bollington: 11ish miles (Taxi back to Leek)
28	Leek to Disley: 25.5 miles	Bollington to Glossop: 17 miles (Taxi to Disley)
29	Disley to Marsden: 23.18 miles	Glossop to Marsden: 17 miles (Taxi to Glossop in the morning)
30	Marsden to Halifax: 12 miles	Marsden to Halifax: 12 miles

As much as we all wanted a day off, if we got up early and got off, we could complete 11 miles before lunch time and then have a good half a day of rest. It was going to be a bit chaotic in terms of getting public transport to and from our new starting points, but it was worth it to make the last few days of walking far more manageable.

As we talked through our plans, I checked my feet only to discover 5 new blisters had graced me with their presence. I just let out a laugh at how ridiculous the situation was. I followed normal protocol and covered them up. After having torn so much skin off removing 'Compeed' the day before, I decided to leave my plasters in place however, I did manage to clean up the liquid seeping out of each blister. The only tape I removed was that on my little toe to allow me to clean the infection with TCP. Since discovering the infection, I was just covering it with gauze and KT tape, which made it easily accessible on 'breaks' rather than the 'Compeed' which was agony to take off.

It really felt like we were on the home stretch now and the next morning we were all in good spirits. We only had 16 miles to walk to get to Leek and if we got a move on, we could have a well-earned rest before setting out again in the evening.

My feet seemed to be getting new blisters by the minute wearing walking boots, so I made the decision that morning to wear my trainers. We got rid of our original route on the Garmin in favour of consulting and following god (aka 'google' maps) instead. We discovered most of our walking would be on roads (rather than wet and soggy footpaths) if we did this which would allow me to walk in my trainers.

On route I had a phone call from my Dad, who had the day off work and was going to drive over to meet us and provide some much-needed support. That was great news and lifted my spirits even more.

It was a tough start to the day with a long walk up a huge incline towards Alton Towers Theme Park. Only months earlier I had visited this park with my friend James from work and we had both noticed how steep and windy the road was. How ironic that I was now *walking* up the very same road.

As we closed in on Leek, we rendezvoused with my Dad in a small farming village called Ipstones where we had a bite to eat before arranging to meet him again in Leek. He would then take us to our campsite which was quite a way out of the town and would mean we didn't have to rely on public transport, he would then give us a hand setting up camp etc.

We picked up the pace for the final 7 miles and I could feel my knees starting to ache, we stopped off for a quick 'breather' so I taped them up and put some 'Compeed' on the arch of my right foot. Where Guess what? I discovered yet another blister was forming. When I was walking, I no longer felt the constant pain from my feet. Perhaps I had become so accustomed to it I just blocked it out. Once I stopped it was a different story and I became aware of how sore my feet really were and once we set off again initially, I was very much aware of the pain.

Our route to Leek was up hill and down. We reached Leek having completed our 16.60 miles by 14.00 which for us was good going. Having met up with my Dad, we managed to find a traditional English pub on the high street where we stopped for a good meal. During our meal we consulted our maps to locate somewhere approximately 5 miles away that we could walk to that evening. We decided on a place called Rushton Spencer, a rural town between Leek and Macclesfield in Staffordshire.

Well and truly stuffed with food, we piled into my Dad's car and were driven to our campsite north of Leek. On arrival I greeted the owners who explained due to recent horrible weather they had moved our pitches out of the camping field and into the caravan section. We now had 2 beautifully cut, flat (and mostly importantly) soft pitches. This would make pushing pegs into the ground far easier for us.

I was now pretty quick at getting my tent pitched and camp made and finished. This time all was completed in under 10 minutes. Meanwhile Rachael and Dean were having a nightmare. One of their tent poles had snapped in half at the worse place possible (where the poles slide together) and was now completely useless. My Dad came to the rescue as he gathered some twigs/small branches which he lashed together with KT Tape to form a brace for the pole and just like that their tent was standing. It was a great save, but I could tell Dean and Rachael were pleased this would be our last night sleeping in tents.

We offloaded a few now unnecessary items onto my Dad to take home in the car including the sets of maps we no longer needed; it was a momentous occasion when we realised, we were finally onto our last set of maps.

It had taken us much longer than planned to set up camp and had only a few hours of day light left. As such we grabbed our headtorches and drinks bottles got back in my Dad's car and headed towards Rushton Spencer, without the added weight of the rucksacks on our backs we hoped we would be able to maintain a faster pace and hopefully get back to Leek before it was too dark.

Although 5 miles doesn't seem like a long way when you say it, the journey in the car seemed to take an age. I kept my eyes on the road we were driving down to see if it had a pavement we could walk on, it did for about the first 2.5 miles. This meant we would be able to walk the last 2.5 miles into Leek via the main road but would have to find an alternative for where there was no pavement further back. After a quick consultation with 'god' fortunately I managed to find a route from Rushton Spencer into Leek that would keep us out of harm's way for the first 2.5 miles.

We bid my Dad farewell and thanked him for his help. It had felt great to see a friendly face for the day and most importantly had re-affirmed how near to home and the finish we were.

Initially our route back to Leek followed a dirt track overshadowed by huge trees that blocked most of the light and before we knew it, we were walking by the light of our head torches. I was more aware of the pain in my feet at this point, perhaps it was because we had stopped walking for so long, which had allowed my blisters to fill up with liquid again.

If our drive had taken a while, walking back felt to take an age as we went on and on through the trees before arriving at a road that would lead us back to the main road with the pavement on. For the next hour we walked in single file like a small line of ants, our only light being that from streetlights and passing traffic, and the only sound being from the cars rushing past us. On and on we walked until we eventually came upon a huge roundabout and the bright lights of Leek.

Agreeing this would be an acceptable place to stop we headed to the nearby 'Sainsburys' to buy supplies for our last few days before heading across the road to a Pub. Any hope of having a quick meal went downhill fast as we spent nearly 2 hours waiting for our food to arrive.

Whilst sat waiting for our meals we looked at our plans for the following day which originally had been a 'day off'. We had planned to cover the 11 miles to Bollington and then return to Leek for the night by taxi as we had already paid for 2 nights camping at the site. However, we decided to revise this plan after all this was meant to be a day off and if we were going have to walk for some of it, we did at least deserve to have the other half of the day in relative comfort. We unanimously agreed to try to find a B&B or hotel where we could stay in or near Bollington. We managed to secure a last-minute booking at a hotel and then called for an 'uber' to take us back to our campsite in Leek. Our driver was incredibly friendly and laughed out loud when we told him what we were doing because he thought weren't being serious. We struck up a humorous conversation with him, and by the end of our taxi journey he had 'liked our page' on Facebook and already 'liked' a number of our photos by the time we were back at our tents.

It was after 21.00 when we arrived at the campsite, which was a late night for us. I was conscious of the pain in my feet which I needed to address before going to bed. I headed to the toilets and after an hour of painfully ripping skin off, cleaning sores and applying iodine gel I was ready for bed. I left the blisters uncovered for the night wondering if this may help dry them out.

It was another long freezing night of tossing and turning, trying to keep every part of myself inside the sleeping bag to avoid what felt like body parts turning into icicles.

I woke at about 05.00 shivering away, but surprisingly felt quite rested. I collapsed my camp in a record 10 minutes, bundle up all my gear and headed to the warmth of the toilet block for breakfast, changing, and blister sorting. I took my time to clean each blister, applying 'Compeed' and tape in the hope this would be the last time I would need to sort them out, apart from my little toe which would still need cleaning twice daily.

As a walking route, that day was nothing special. We jumped in a taxi back to Rushton Spencer and then spent the rest of the day walking along the side of a main road before cutting off onto tow paths into Bollington. It may have been more boring than walking through fields of cows or poo, but it meant I could walk in the relative comfort of my trainers again rather than wearing my walking boots which would probably have resulted in adding more blisters to my record-breaking collection. The final mile of the day involved a long, long climb up a hill, but we managed to check into our hotel around 16.00 which meant we got a good few hours of well-deserved rest. Once 'checked in' I followed my normal routine of asking for a bucket of ice for my feet which I emptied into the bath and soaked my feet in.

It seemed we had booked ourselves into quite an 'upmarket hotel' when we looked at the evening menu and price list! To keep costs down initially, Dean and I only ordered 'starters' but Rachael was feeling particularly hungry and decided to 'splash the cash', getting herself a main meal. When the food reached the table the look on Rachael's face was priceless! Her 'main meal' was smaller than either starter. We couldn't stop laughing at the sheer stupidity of the situation.

As ever we went to bed early having agreed on a 06.30 breakfast. Just before I dozed off, Rachael dropped me a message to say her Mum had been in touch with 'Look North' (our local TV News Programme) and they had confirmed that they would be at the Piece Hall (our final finishing point in Halifax) and may even do part of the final walk with us. This was based on there being no major breaking news to cover in the area at the same time. We were all over the moon, this was fantastic news and would really help us get the exposure we needed for the challenge to raise more money for charity.

CHAPTER 24: 'TAKE ME HOME, COUNTRY ROAD'

We were early for breakfast the next morning as we waited for staff to set the area up. It was pouring down with rain, but this didn't lower our moral; we were still buzzing from being told to expect 'Look North' at the Piece Hall.

We wrapped ourselves up in every waterproof layer we had and set out into the rain. It didn't take long for us to get soaked through as the rain hammered down for hours on end. My trainers were drenched but thankfully my waterproof socks kept my feet dry however I did make a lovely squelching noise each step I took.

At one point we stooped for a quick breather under a bridge, rain was pouring off us as we laughed and joked about the situation. I looked down at Rachael's waterproof trousers that seemed to be foaming. Whatever they had been washed with previously was now coming out of the trousers with the rain and her legs were turning white, it looked hilarious.

We kept to paths and roads as much as possible, so I didn't have to wear my walking boots again and this was doing wonders for my feet. While I could still feel pain on every step, I was no longer getting new blisters and the swelling gradually seemed to be decreasing. Result!!!

My Mum had been in touch to say she would meet us at our lunch stop and take my walking boots off me to switch them for the walking shoes I had worn in France. This would mean I would be better prepared for the mud and bogs we would no doubt be walking through during the last few days.

We made it to the small town of Marple, that lies along the Peak Forest Canal, absolutely drenched from head to toe where we piled into a small café for lunch. We took over the full reception area of the place with our bags and gear as we tried as much as possible to spread things out to dry.

My Mum arrived around 20 minutes later, so we ordered food which we dragged out as long as possible in the hope that our clothes may dry off. They did, a bit.

As we left the café the rain eased up slightly, I changed into my walking shoes and left my sodden trainers in my Mum's car in the hope they would dry out next to the heater. My Mum volunteered to meet us at the other end of our walk when she would then drive us to our hotel. We had now reached the point in our journey where we were completely across with where we were finishing our days and where we were staying at night, in fact at that point Disley (our stop for the night) was several miles south of our current position, so having someone to pick us up instead of having to rely on taxis was going to be a great help.

It stayed dry for the rest of the day and was a pleasant walk up over the hills and into Glossop. When we actually saw a signpost for Sheffield, somewhere we actually knew, it was an amazing feeling. It felt WE WERE NEAR HOME! We checked in to our hotel for the night absolutely thrilled with the knowledge that we only had two days walking left. Although given that our final day would only be 12 miles long and we would be done alongside friends and family we had previously agreed that this didn't actually count as a day. WE ONLY HAD ONE DAY LEFT.

By now everything we did came naturally to us in term of taping our feet, packing our bags or just putting our head down and walking. It felt as though we had one purpose in life or one job to do and that was to walk.

It was now our final day (well by our counting system), really it was our penultimate day) and I woke up feeling motivated and ready to go. I knew it was going to be quite tough as we had a big climb ahead of us through the Peak District before dropping into Marsden, but we were nearly there and not even the pain in my feet was going to dampen my mood.

A friend of the family called Sue had arranged to meet us that morning and walk with us for the day, a keen walker herself Sue knew the way to Marsden and had agreed to show us the way. It was lovely to have different company and it made the day go that much faster. It was a long tough climb to the top of Black Hill which involved crossing open moorland, successfully negotiating marshland, with some time spent walking on gravel pathways and despite this mixture we were able to maintain a regular and fast pace. Our most challenging obstacles were undoubtedly the numerous bogs and streams in the valleys of the open moorland. Unfortunately for me I succumbed to one of the bogs when my foot sank down into a deep quagmire of mud and peat. Thankfully, I emerged with my shoe intact and we laughed it off as I changed my socks to a dry pair, at least it wasn't quite a repeat of 'poo gate'.

We arrived into Marsden to find it bustling with people, there was some form of festival going on and everywhere was packed. Again, we stood out like a sore thumb meandering our way through the streets in our walking gear. My mum was on pick up duty, but it took us a long time to meet up due to parking being a nightmare. We popped into one of the local cafes for some hot drinks and a relax. I felt a huge sense of relief and achievement, for me the main part of the challenge was now over. All that was left was a short 12-mile day surrounded by my friends and family, with a finish that was going to culminate in potential interviews with the local news and radio stations. That being said 12 miles was still 12 miles and an early night was needed to prepare myself for the final slog.

A little time for here for reflection if I may.

Had someone said to me before we undertook the 'Quest for Brest Challenge' do you fancy going for a 12 mile walk tomorrow over open moorland. In boots/shoes that are incredibly uncomfortable, with feet already sore, and on a day when rain was guaranteed, I doubt I would have responded enthusiastically or with any relief.

How far had the three/sometimes 4 of us come along our epic journey both mentally and emotionally. The walk the next day would be different. We would be part of larger group of walkers some of whom would be undertaking such a distance for the first time, others who walked regularly and felt confident. Others who would put their heart and soul into the walk and drain themselves of every ounce of energy to accomplish it. There would be some amongst us who would need help, the next day would prove to be a challenge of a different type.

That night my parents' house turned into 'Quest for Brest Headquarters' as we all descended on it to eat and sleep. Family were arriving from further north to join us on the walk next day and everything was a bit chaotic. Being suddenly surrounded by so many people all at once after such a long period of it being just the 3 of us was lovely but also very overwhelming and exhausting and as the hours went by all I wanted was my bed. At around 23.00 (4 hours later than normal) I was finally able to go to sleep.

CHAPTER 25: ONE DAY MORE

So, the time had arrived, it was our final day, the final 12 miles, one last push and we would be finished.

To say the morning was a bit crazy was an understatement.

We had been used to just the 3 or 4 of us being up bright and early and on our way within an hour or so of waking up. Now it was different, we had a house full of people to ferry out of the door and onto the train to Marsden. With 7 people in a house with only 1 bathroom it was chaos as we frantically rushed around sorting food and preparing ourselves for the day ahead. Soon enough our taxis arrived to take us to the train station in Huddersfield to catch our train to Marsden. We made it on time and as we headed to our platform all loaded up with walking rucksacks, we bumped into Sue who would be joining us once more with her husband Allen.

At 9.40 we pulled into Marsden train station and just as we stepped off the train it began to rain, not heavily but enough to be noticed.

Over the next 5 minutes or so our crowd of walkers got bigger and bigger until there was over 20 of us standing in a huddle on the bridge. Uncles, Aunties, Cousins and a number of extended family and friends had come to join us despite the rain. Even though we knew there would have been even more if the weather had been kinder to us, I was thankful to all those who had turned up ready to take on the challenge.

It was 9.45 and time to set off but couldn't as we were expecting more people to join us. We had a finishing time at the Piece Hall of 16.00 so we really needed to get a move on. What a dilemma? Do we set off and risk the chance of disappointing those who were already late or set off in the hope that they would be able to catch us up at some point.

In the knowledge that we had a tight time frame to stick to a few of the group set off including my Mum and brother. The route out of Marsden included a mile of steep incline that would prove challenging to my Brother who has Autism and severe learning and communication needs. He would need extra time to negotiate paths, obstacles and stiles that others find relatively easy to overcome so they set off ahead hoping they could take their time before the full group took to the hills making underfoot even more difficult to negotiate.

That was the last I saw of them for hours.

As the last of those to join us arrived we set off in the same general direction as the earlier group had gone. A line of 20+ people now began to climb the banking, with it getting more and more slippy with every step. I was near the front and Steve (Phil's day/my father in law) was bringing up the rear with a huge Yorkshire flag strapped to his rucksack. My calves were on fire by the time I got to the top of the hill.

It didn't take long for it to dawn on me that this plan had been terrible. The only people who knew where we were meant to be going were in the group a good few miles in front of us. Thank fully I had phone signal so once up the hill I phoned my Mum for directions as I arrived at a cross roads, I then passed the information back down the line and continued on in the hope of bridging the gap between the front group and the rest of us.

Our route flattened out and we began to make our way over open moorland and our group became more and more splintered as all the different walking paces became apparent. I knew this was going to be the case, but I hadn't expected to become so quickly apparent. I was still clinging to the hope that most of the walk would be achieved as a single group however in reality this was not going to happen.

Within 30 minutes of setting off my Mum and brother were now several miles ahead of me, Phil, Jackie and Steve were some distance behind me, and I was in the middle unsure of what to do and how to keep everyone together. We carried on and on in the drizzle and incoming fog, struggling to see our fellow walkers behind us, in fact I hadn't seen Phil since we set off in Marsden and as it turned out I wouldn't see him again for most of the day.

We continued on as the rain got heavier and the ground more and more muddy. At one point we were actually walking on the top of a crumbled dry-stone wall just to keep ourselves on sturdy ground. I spent the time talking to various members of my family as they passed me, or I caught up with them.

Our group continued to break up and were soon in 4 groups all walking at different paces. I had thankfully managed to catch up with my Mum and brother who had broken off from the front but lost Dean and Rachael who un beknown to me had stopped to talk to someone they knew on route.

We soon came to a main road which I didn't realise was one I have driven over many times, the A640 also known as New Hey Road. Such was the weather and mist I had no idea where I was or that we were so close to our first check point, Scammonden Reservoir.

Our route now followed quite a steep descent towards the reservoir which I eventually recognized as Scammonden. At this point I quickly checked my watch to find by my calculations we were only around 10 minutes behind schedule, so I was filled with hope that we may all be able to stop and let those behind us catch up.

I soon got a phone call from Phil who was still with the group at the rear, they had made it across the moors but weren't sure where to go from there, I tried to describe to them the path they needed to take to make it down into the valley and as I hung up Dean and Rachael appeared, I had completely lost track of where they were and could have sworn they were in front of me.

As a three we made our way into the bottom of the valley where my Mum and Brother were waiting for us, we then stood with our eyes fixed on the top of the banking we had just come down waiting to see if Phil and the rest of his group had managed to pick up the correct route.

It wasn't long before we saw a group of figures appear over the top of the ridge and I could make out Phil's bright orange coat amongst them, the problem was they were heading in the completely wrong direction trying to navigate their way down a boggy field with no real path to it. I watched on helplessly as they continued to veer off course. I rang Phil back to re explain the route and tell him that we would carry on with the aim of meeting up with the front group, to try and get them to wait for everyone, after all they were only probably about 10 minutes behind us now.

We found the front group at our meeting point, sat in a tunnel under the motorway eating their lunch. They had been there some time, had managed to take a break and were getting ready to set off again. I tried to explain the situation we had found ourselves in, that the walking party had become several walking parties. Those of us who had just arrived at the check point needed to eat, have a toilet stop of some form and have a short break. My attempts to delay the front group setting off were fruitless at that point. They were eager to get on their way (understandably so) and that bit nearer to the end. So, I together with a cluster of other walkers sat to eat our lunch as the first group made their way down the embankment of Scammonden Dam before disappearing completely out of sight.

I was gutted. This was not how I had hoped this day would be. I knew it would be hard for everyone to stay together but I had not expected it to be like this. I felt torn as I was now in a position where if I stayed behind there was a good chance I wouldn't make it to the Piece Hall in time for the big finish at 16.30 and I would miss being there with my Mum who this whole challenge was for, but then on the other hand if I carried on I would be leaving Phil (who was not only my husband but an integral part of the team behind the whole idea of "Quest for Brest") unable to make it to the finish point either. I was in a no-win situation and felt helpless.

It's funny how often something just happens to lighten your mood this time in the form of "comic relief". We had to make our way down the other side of Scammonden Reservoir which was I quite a steep and muddy decline. I watched my Mum and Brother start to make their way down slowly, but it wasn't long before my brother lost his footing completely and slid down the banking. He got up immediately, totally oblivious that his coat was completely covered in mud and was ready to set off again. Although my brother is Autistic he has a very cheeky personality and had that been me who had fallen he would never have let me forget it (even in 20 years-time he would still be reminding me of the incident) So, I took my opportunity to do what every younger sister should do in this situation and rib him for it.

'Joe, did you fall over' I asked him jokingly.

'No, Joe didn't fall over' he quickly replied.

I asked him if he didn't fall over why was he covered in mud. He couldn't give me an answer and instead shrugged his shoulders, I explained it was okay to have fallen over and that he could laugh about it. With Joe now covered in mud we carried on.

We made it to the bottom of Scammonden Dam and having continued to walk some distance had managed to meet up with some of the walkers that had gone ahead. We had another short stop off for a snack and once again pleaded with the group that we rest longer to allow Phil and the others to get within a reasonable distance of us. I managed to stall us long enough to make out Phil's coat on the horizon. Concerned that Phil and his group of walkers had no real route guide to follow, Stacey, a family friend, took one of our route cards and began heading back in Phil and company's direction to try and help them find their way quicker.

The main group once again set off walking towards our next meeting point.

It continued on like this for the next 5 miles as I walked along side different groups of people before losing site of them and joining with the next group.

At the halfway point it was just me, with my Brother (still covered in mud but totally oblivious of this) and my Mum walking with no one else to be seen. My Mum was complaining of some discomfort in her left foot around her big toe. As a newly self-crowned blister expert I told her to get her shoes off so I could take a look. This short pause in proceedings allowed a few others to catch us up and there was now a group of 5 of us walking together. We managed to stay like this up to our 3rd and final check point of the day before the finish, a local garden centre.

On arrival I saw another large group of people who had come along to walk with us including some more of my cousins and uncles. I popped into the garden centre for a much-needed loo break and no sooner had I started walking back to the group, everyone began moving off. I rang Phil again to see how far behind his group were, the good news was that they were gaining on us but were still a couple of miles behind.

We were scheduled to arrive at the Piece Hall between 16.00 and 16.30, and with the chance of the local news and radio stations being there we could not be late as we knew they wouldn't stick around. It was nearly 16.00 as I stood watching everyone begin to leave the garden centre and we still had 2 miles to go.

I rang my Dad who was coordinating proceedings at the Piece Hall to tell him we would probably be late arriving; it was more likely to be 16.30 than 16.00 and how we were all completely split up. He said he would try and keep everyone entertained and occupied to buy us a bit more time, but as it was still raining this wasn't going to be an easy job. He also offered to drive to where Phil and his group of walkers were to pick them up and move them along the route to us so they wouldn't miss out on the big finish.

While all this was going on I suddenly realised Dean and Rachael were still stood in the car park of the garden centre. I felt a slight sense of relief, 3 out of the 4 of us that had started out this journey in France were together, we now just needed Phil. I rang him up again and explained my Dad's offer, but he wouldn't take it and told me to just finish it and he would see me afterwards.

I was feeling frustrated, confused and disappointed. From day one I had wanted the final day to be about everyone coming together to complete this momentous journey surrounded by my friends and family. Cancer doesn't just affect the immediate family of those diagnosed it has an effect on the whole family and I wanted us to all cross the line together. I had to resign myself to the fact that this wasn't going to be the actual reality, far from it!

Thankfully my Mum and Brother were still with me as were Judith and Derek, Phil's Auntie and Uncle, they all suggested they stay back to wait for the others and show them the way as my Mum had done a practice walk only the week before and was familiar with the route. I pleaded with my Mum to continue on with me, so if the situation arouse and we had to finish without the others by our side she could at least be there. She said I had to set off and that she would follow on once she had explained directions for the rest of the route to Judith and Derek to relay to the others behind.

I set off at the slowest pace possible to allow my Mum and Brother to catch up in the knowledge that at least with Dean and Rachael by my side the celebrations wouldn't be able to start until we arrived at the Piece Hall regardless of whether others arrived before us. So, we continued on for our last 2 miles knowing we now only had around 25 minutes left to get there.

We hit the 1 mile to go marker as we were walking on the Calder and Hebble trail. Joined by a family friend Craig, we came across a small park with exercise machines and had a laugh while playing on them. Thankfully this short stop allowed my Mum and Brother to catch us up and we continued on. We soon passed a group of new houses where their foundations were being supported by scaffolding. Recent flooding in our area had completely decimated the foundations some of which could be seen in the River Calder.

We picked up our walking pace as we began to make our way off the Calder and Hebble Trail and up towards the main road which would then lead us straight to the Piece Hall. It was at this point that I got another phone call from Phil. When I answered he sounded completely out of breath.

'Where are you guys?' he said gasping.

I told him our location.

'Awesome I'm just stood at the bottom of that road'

What. Only 20 minutes ago he had been at least two miles behind us if not more.

It turned out that once he had put the phone down earlier, he had decided the only way he could catch us up was to run the rest of the way. So, with a rucksack weighing at least 12kg on his back he had run like a madman for 2 miles to try and catch us before we got to the Piece Hall. Annoyingly for him he hadn't known what route we were taking so had run along the main roads, including up a well know hill (Salterhebble for you Elland/Halifax folk) instead of cutting along the Calder and Hebble Trail we had used with very little incline.

Poor Phil. He sounded exhausted.

He explained that the others in his group wanted to finish the miles but would be unlikely to make it to the finish point in time. I was gutted but respected their decision as I knew a number of them were using this 12-mile walk as an opportunity to collect sponsorship money for Macmillan as well as part of our cause so we couldn't expect them to give up their own personal challenge. From the point that Phil had left them we guesstimated that they may be around 10 minutes behind, so we hatched a plan.

We had 10 minutes before we were due to arrive at the Piece Hall. We would continue on and just before our arrival we would stop off for 5 minutes, change into our white 'final day' t-shirts (with them being white we hadn't wanted them to get covered in mud during the day) in the hope that this may give them some chance to catch up.

We dragged out our changing stop for as long as possible, but it was now after 16.30 and we were more than overdue at the Piece Hall. We needed to keep moving. I took one final look behind us in the hope of seeing a giant Yorkshire flag highlighting the location of the group behind us but there was no one there.

I looked over at Phil, Dean and Rachael, this was it, we were now no more than 200 metres away from the end of this incredible journey. It felt surreal. That whole day had been such a mixed wave of emotions, trying to keep everyone together and constantly worrying about where everyone was that I had to take a second to try and bring myself back into the moment and appreciate what was about to happen.

All 4 of us set off once more with my Mum and Brother and as we approached the Piece Hall, we could hear the commotion inside. As we walked closer, we began to quickly reminisce about what we had all been through to get to this point, the highs, the lows and how at many points it had felt like we may never make it.

We turned the corner and began to walk towards the entrance of the Piece Hall where we could hear the sounds of cheers and clapping. I saw my Dad with the biggest grin on his face walking under the arched entrance towards us as we were suddenly surrounded by friends and family wanting to take our pictures.

My Dad asked us to pause outside briefly as they were having as few technical difficulties with the PA and music system that would announce our arrival. This worked well for us as we hoped it may give the others a chance to catch up.

We waited desperately for around 10 minutes as I was given a pair of scissors to cut the ribbon for our big finish. My Dad then came and told us that he was sorry, but we could wait no longer as everything was ready, and it was time to make our entrance.

Seconds later the town crier began to shake his bell to get everyone's attention, as I heard his voice fill the air I knew that was our cue, we gave one last hopeful look down the road to see if there was any sign of the others, but it was hopeless.

Side by side we proceeded under the arch way and into the wide-open square of the Piece Hall, crowds of people had lined our route like a guard of honour, with many more on the upper balcony clapping and waving. I think had the day not been so draining I may have just burst into tears, instead I felt numb and gobsmacked as to how many people had turned up.

As I heard our names bellowed out by the town crier, I began to make out some familiar faces in the crowd. It felt strange to be the centre of attention and in many ways very uncomfortable, I just set my sights on the ribbon set across the top of the lines of people and carried on moving forwards.

Step by step we were edging closer.

I held the scissors out in front of me and cut the ribbon.

As we stepped over the line, I raised my arm into the air and gave out a small cheer. It was over, we had done it, we had walked home from France.

CHAPTER 26: THE END

What happened after that was all a bit of a blur as friends and family descended on us. We were handed medals by Macmillan representatives as the Proclaimers '500 miles' began to blare over the speaker system.

I managed to seek out my Mum in all the chaos and just pulled her in for a hug, while trying to hold back the tears. I was so proud of her; she had not only battled through the past year, but she had just completed a 12 mile walk only months on from finishing her treatment. Next I found my Dad and squeezed him tightly.

I continued to hug and talk to what felt like every member of the local community as everyone came over to congratulate me. I struggled to keep track of who everyone was but every so often I could see a smiling face of someone I recognised.

As the four of us stood around chatting, a small group of young lads had come over to see what was going on. Someone in the crowd explained to them what we had done but they refused to believe it, simply stating that it's not possible to walk across the channel (which to be fair is true). Instead they told everyone that we had probably just jumped on the train up from London. We laughed it off and bid them farewell.

As soon as I had a second to spare, I threw off my walking shoes, it had only really occurred to me on stopping how much my feet were throbbing, and it was such a relief to be free of them.

What happened next was probably one of the strangest occurrences of all.

My eyes were drawn to a crowd that had surrounded themselves around Dean and a gentleman with his back to me that he was talking to, I made my way over there to see what was going on.

Unbelievably the mystery gentleman was none other than Jon Richardson the well know British comedian and he was now stood in the Piece Hall in Halifax casually having a chat to Dean. What?

Before I knew it, I was in conversation with a celebrity. He congratulated us on our fantastic achievement and happily posed for a few photographs before heading on his way. Apparently, he was in Halifax to buy some new walking boots (the irony) and had wondered what the commotion was and come over to find out.

It turned out we had been let down by the TV and Radio companies who failed to show after promising us they would be there. We felt a sense of disappointment but having Jon Richardson drop in our celebrations more than made up for it.

Celebrations continued as I was introduced to a variety of different people all passing on their congratulations. I was moving about the crowds trying to say hello to everyone I knew and thank them for their support.

As the crowds slowly died off, we were left surrounded by family and friends and as the 4 of us stood in the middle of it all we shared a big group hug. Everyone soon began to congregate for a big group picture and as a Macmillan banner was raised aloft, I felt my self-grinning from ear to ear, we had done it.

Up yours Cancer!

CHAPTER 27: EPILOGUE

So, time has passed on our adventure and I sit here typing this a year to the date of us setting off. I always hoped I would have this book out and onto the shelves a lot earlier than this, but life has its way of scuppering your plans.

I spent my first few days following the completion of the walk resting and recovering as much as possible. As a team we booked ourselves in for a spa day and enjoyed the down time that followed. Life soon returned back to normal, but the physical scars took a while to heal.

I lost a few toenails and my feet definitely changed shape as I could no longer fit my feet into any of my shoes at home. The blisters healed slowly, and they still flare up regularly now if I walk any kind of distance.

We raised over £6000 for Macmillan Cancer Support and while this is a fantastic amount, I'm still on a mission to raise more.

Ending the walk surrounded by family and friends, particularly my Mum felt like some form of closure on our run in with cancer. My Mum was recovering well, and things were really starting to look up.

Then in January of this year (2020) the 'c word' reared its ugly head again and this time it was terminal. Anger, frustration and downright helplessness are just some of the feelings I had on hearing my Mum's cancer had returned. Ever the optimist my Mum didn't want to let it get her down and we even joked that I wasn't going to be walking anywhere this time.

I now sit here in October of 2020 amidst the 'Covid 19' pandemic trying to come to terms with the fact that my mum has just been told nothing else can be done for her now and time is running out.

It just proves that cancer knows no limits and won't hesitate to strike again. My Mum is one of the strongest people I know and if I could walk home from France every month to stop her and others suffering from this horrible disease I would.

For now, I am going to focus all my energy into doing every bit I can to raise more money to help Macmillan Cancer Support so even though I can't save my mum I can do my bit to help others. If you wish to donate our webpage is still live at www.questforbrest.com where there is a link to our just giving page.

I thank you from the bottom of my heart for purchasing and reading this book. I know for certain this won't be the last challenge I do, cancer has made this incredibly personal and while it may be winning the battle at the moment and taking away our loved ones I refuse to stand by idly when I could do more to help.

So, keep your eyes peeled, but mostly importantly…who wants to join me on my next challenge?

Printed in Poland
by Amazon Fulfillment
Poland Sp. z o.o., Wrocław

63050954R00075